MY EYES ARE UP HERE

BY RYAN SOHMER & LAR DESOUZA

LEAST I COULD DO
VOLUME THREE

Blind Ferret Entertainment © 2009

Least I Could Do is distributed by Blind Ferret Entertainment.

First paperback edition published 2009.

www.leasticoulddo.com

ISBN 978-0-9812163-5-5

Book Credits
Written by Ryan Sohmer
Strips by Lar deSouza
Book Layout and Cover by Lar deSouza

For Blind Ferret Entertainment

Randy Waxman - President & CEO
Ryan Sohmer - Vice President, Creative Director
Marc Aflalo - Media Director & Public Relations Manager
Lar DeSouza - Art Director

MARC ANTHONY!

URF! UNF!
HUF! HUF!
I DON'T KNOW WHAT CONVENIENCE STORE YOU STOLE THAT FROM, BUT YOU SHOULD PROBABLY KNOW THAT IT'S PLASTIC AND NOT ACTUALLY FILLED WITH RED BULL.
Red Bull

PRIORITIES

COME ON, RAYNE,
WE'VE GOT A LOT OF WORK TO DO BEFORE THE DINNER TOMORROW.
I'LL BE RIGHT WITH YOU AS SOON AS I FINISH THIS CASE.
WHAT'RE YOU-
LET'S GO *NOW.*
I'M GONNA TELL JESUS ON YOU.
TELL HIM HOW MUCH YOU LOVE ABORTIONS AND KICKING THE HOMELESS.
THAT'LL LEARN YOU.

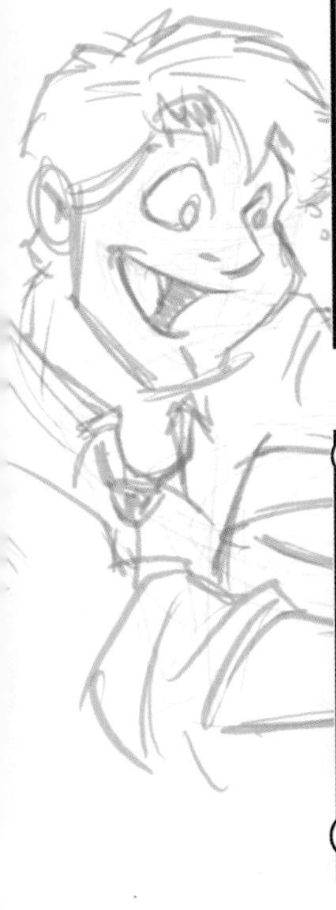

CHARITY BEGINS AT RAYNE

DO YOU THINK WE SHOULD SERVE THE VEAL OR THE DUCK?
TWELVE.
YOU'RE SUPPOSED TO BE HELPING ME HERE. ARE YOU EVEN LISTENING TO ANYTHING I SAY?
NOT EVEN THE LITTLEST OF BITS.
THE DINNER IS TOMORROW–
...I'VE HAD ENOUGH.
IT'S ALL UP TO YOU NOW.
YOU CAN DO IT ALL.
I'LL GIVE YOU ONE GUESS AS TO WHAT SHE SHOULDN'T HAVE JUST SAID.
READY?
GO.

BUSINESS CLASSY

WHERE ARE YOU?
ON MY WAY BACK INTO TOWN.
I LAND WITHIN THE HOUR.
HOW ARE THINGS GOING FOR TONIGHT?
ARE YOU AND EMMA GETTING ALONG?
WELL ENOUGH, I SUPPOSE.
BECAUSE OF MY CHARITABLE SPIRIT AND GENEROUS SOUL, SHE'S DECIDED TO LEAVE ALL THE PLANNING TO ME.
SHOULD I BE BRINGING A HORDE OF LAWYERS WITH ME, OR THE FIRE MARSHAL?
A COUPLE GUYS IN HAZMAT SUITS WOULDN'T BE AMISS, EITHER.
LISTEN, I GOTTA GO.
THE RATS ARE HERE.
CAN I GET YOU ANYTHING, MS MCKEAN?
TWELVE SHOTS OF BOURBON AND AN OFFER TO PURCHASE MY MAJORITY STOCK IN IDS WOULD BE WONDERFUL.
THANK YOU.

DEFENDING YOUR RIGHT TO PARTY

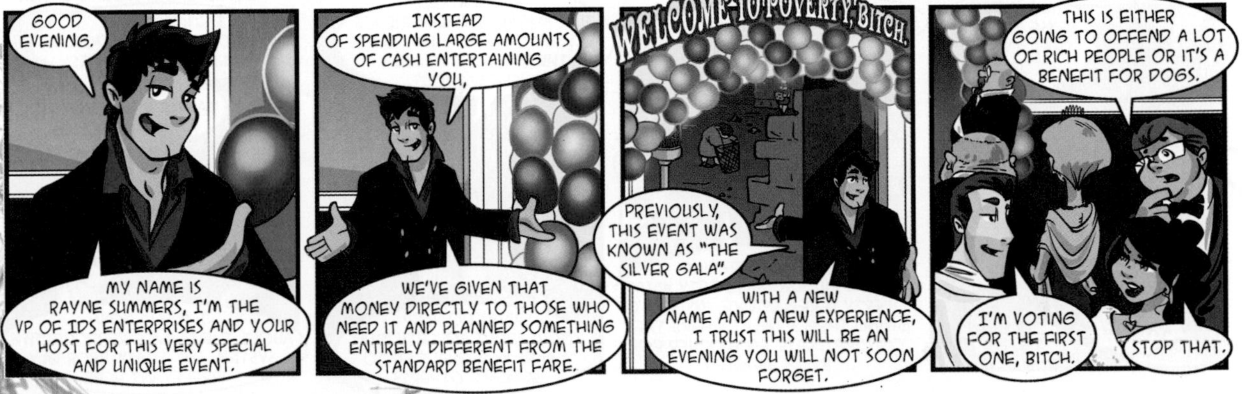

GOOD EVENING.
MY NAME IS RAYNE SUMMERS, I'M THE VP OF IDS ENTERPRISES AND YOUR HOST FOR THIS VERY SPECIAL AND UNIQUE EVENT.
INSTEAD OF SPENDING LARGE AMOUNTS OF CASH ENTERTAINING YOU,
WE'VE GIVEN THAT MONEY DIRECTLY TO THOSE WHO NEED IT AND PLANNED SOMETHING ENTIRELY DIFFERENT FROM THE STANDARD BENEFIT FARE.
WELCOME TO POVERTY, BITCH.
PREVIOUSLY, THIS EVENT WAS KNOWN AS "THE SILVER GALA".
WITH A NEW NAME AND A NEW EXPERIENCE, I TRUST THIS WILL BE AN EVENING YOU WILL NOT SOON FORGET.
THIS IS EITHER GOING TO OFFEND A LOT OF RICH PEOPLE OR IT'S A BENEFIT FOR DOGS.
I'M VOTING FOR THE FIRST ONE, BITCH.
STOP THAT.

EMPTY PIZZA BOXES ARE A GOOD SOURCE OF CHEESE

MR. SUMMERS! MR. SUMMERS!
YES, ARCHIE?
MY MOTHER'S PURSE WAS JUST STOLEN BY A MAN WEARING A GARBAGE BAG FOR PANTS.
ALL PART OF THE NIGHTS FESTIVITIES.
I SEE.
WILL HER PURSE BE RETURNED TO HER?
PROBABLY NOT.
IT'S ALL ABOUT THE REALISM TONIGHT.
I DON'T THINK SHE'S GOING TO ENJOY HERSELF.
I'D ADVISE STEERING CLEAR OF THE HOBOS WITH THE BATS, THEN.
THEY WERE TOLD NOT TO GO EASY.
BY ME.

GREAT POWER COMES

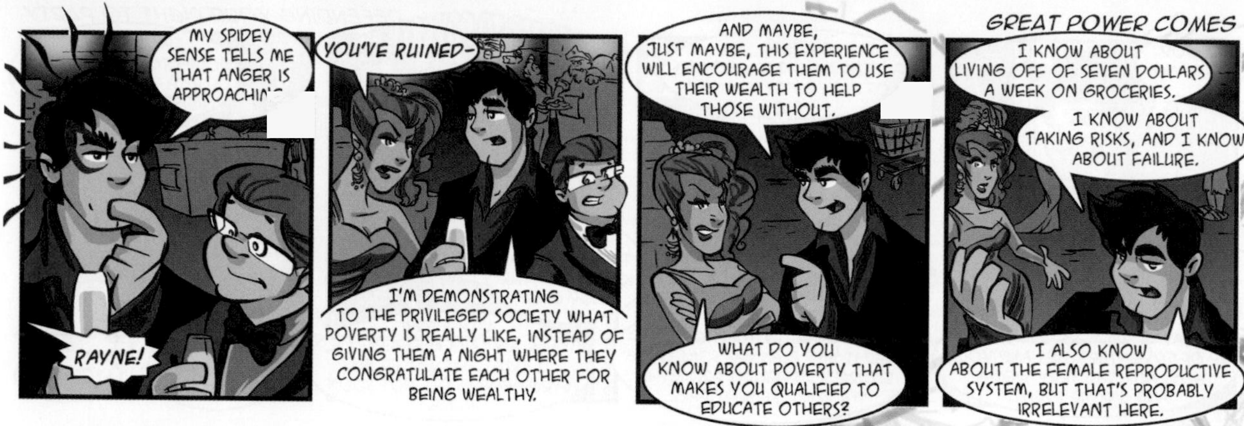

MY SPIDEY SENSE TELLS ME THAT ANGER IS APPROACHIN-
RAYNE!
YOU'VE RUINED-
I'M DEMONSTRATING TO THE PRIVILEGED SOCIETY WHAT POVERTY IS REALLY LIKE, INSTEAD OF GIVING THEM A NIGHT WHERE THEY CONGRATULATE EACH OTHER FOR BEING WEALTHY.
AND MAYBE, JUST MAYBE, THIS EXPERIENCE WILL ENCOURAGE THEM TO USE THEIR WEALTH TO HELP THOSE WITHOUT.
WHAT DO YOU KNOW ABOUT POVERTY THAT MAKES YOU QUALIFIED TO EDUCATE OTHERS?
I KNOW ABOUT LIVING OFF OF SEVEN DOLLARS A WEEK ON GROCERIES.
I KNOW ABOUT TAKING RISKS, AND I KNOW ABOUT FAILURE.
I ALSO KNOW ABOUT THE FEMALE REPRODUCTIVE SYSTEM, BUT THAT'S PROBABLY IRRELEVANT HERE.

RESURRERECTION

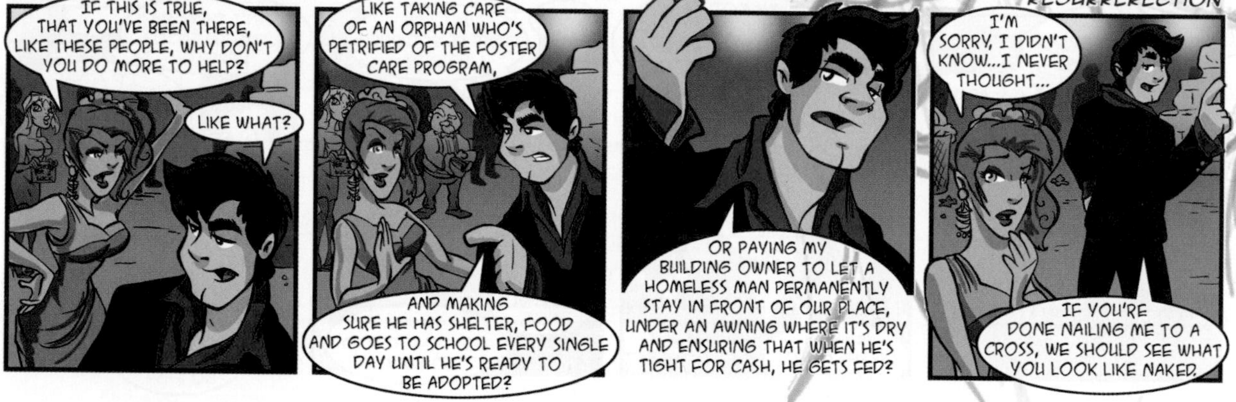

IF THIS IS TRUE, THAT YOU'VE BEEN THERE, LIKE THESE PEOPLE, WHY DON'T YOU DO MORE TO HELP?
LIKE WHAT?
LIKE TAKING CARE OF AN ORPHAN WHO'S PETRIFIED OF THE FOSTER CARE PROGRAM,
AND MAKING SURE HE HAS SHELTER, FOOD AND GOES TO SCHOOL EVERY SINGLE DAY UNTIL HE'S READY TO BE ADOPTED?
OR PAYING MY BUILDING OWNER TO LET A HOMELESS MAN PERMANENTLY STAY IN FRONT OF OUR PLACE, UNDER AN AWNING WHERE IT'S DRY AND ENSURING THAT WHEN HE'S TIGHT FOR CASH, HE GETS FED?
I'M SORRY, I DIDN'T KNOW...I NEVER THOUGHT...
IF YOU'RE DONE NAILING ME TO A CROSS, WE SHOULD SEE WHAT YOU LOOK LIKE NAKED.

STILL LIFE

HELLO.
MAY I HELP YOU?
I WAS JUST SAYING HELLO, LADY.
MY FAMILY IS WORTH MILLIONS,
YOUR NET WORTH IS MOST LIKELY LOCATED IN YOUR USED JACKET POCKET.
WE HAVE NOTHING TO SAY TO EACH OTHER.
CAN I DRAW YOU A PICTURE?
I'M NOT GIVING YOU ANY MONEY FOR IT.
I DO ART BECAUSE I LOVE IT AND FOR NO OTHER REASON.
NOW, WOULD YOU PREFER TO BE ON ROLLER-SKATES ON A BRIGHT SUNNY DAY,
OR SODOMIZED BY A KLINGON?
YOU KNOW WHAT? I'LL CHOOSE.

CHECKMATE

YOU MADE IT!
THERE ARE A FEW MEDIA OUTLETS, LOCAL AND NATIONAL, THAT WANT A FEW MINUTES OF YOUR TIME FOR AN INTERVIEW.
YOU WANTED TO MAKE AN IMPACT WITH THIS THING, AND THAT'S WHAT WE DID.
ANYTIME YOU WANT TO EXPRESS YOUR DELIGHT, GO AHEAD.
I JUST SAW ONE OF OUR BOARD MEMBERS PLAYING CHESS WITH A WOMAN COVERED IN PIGEON CRAP WHO KEPT MAKING BIRD SOUNDS EVERY TIME SHE TOUCHED A PIECE.
CAN THAT BE OUR NEW SLOGAN?

THINK GLOBALLY. ACT LIKE RAYNE

YOU DID A GOOD JOB TONIGHT.
RAISED SOME DECENT COIN, AND DISTRIBUTED A LOT OF FOOD TO MY VOLUNTEERS.
EMMA STILL WOULDN'T COME HOME WITH ME THOUGH, DESPITE THE GREAT LINE I HAD SAVED UP FOR TONIGHT.
I'LL BITE.
ONCE THE INTERCOURSE HAD BEGUN, I WAS GOING TO TAKE A JESUS LIKE POSE AND UTTER THE WORDS:
"THE KINGDOM OF HEAVEN IS WITHIN YOU"
YOU WERE GOING TO REFER TO YOUR PENIS AS 'THE KINGDOM OF HEAVEN'
LOOKS THAT WAY.
CONGRATULATIONS.
YOU JUST NEUTRALIZED YOUR CHARITABLE WORKS IN RECORD TIME.
I KNEW YOU WERE KEEPING SCORE.

YOINK

HE'S GOING TO CATCH US!
RELAX.
JUST A LITTLE FURTHER AND WE'RE OUT OF HIS JURISDICTION.
THWIP
HEY!
YEAH...
I'LL..UHHH,
CATCH YOU GUYS WHEN YOU'RE BACK IN THE CITY.
COOL.

EASIER THAN GETTING A PASSPORT

WHY DID I GET SENT AN APPLICATION FOR PERMANENT DISABILITY FROM THE GOVERNMENT?
BECAUSE I REQUESTED IT.
WHY?
BECAUSE I'M A GOOD FRIEND AND I WANT TO SEE YOU HAPPY.
HE EVEN STARTED FILLING THEM OUT FOR YOU.
YOU WROTE THAT I'M A EUNUCH.
THAT'S WHAT IT SAYS.
GOING TO TELL HIM THAT YOU SENT A COPY TO HIS SCHOOL FOR THEM TO CONFIRM?
NOT UNTIL HE SAYS 'THANK YOU.'
SLAM

FOOT LONG

MY EYES ARE UP HERE.
BUT YOUR BREASTS ARE DOWN THERE.
MY EYES...
ARE UP THERE. YES, I KNOW.
I'LL GET TO THEM IN A MINUTE.
I'M SURE THEY'RE LOVELY.
AND THAT'S WHY WE CAN'T GO INTO THAT SUBWAY ANYMORE.
MY EYES ARE UP HERE.

BETWEEN FIVE, IT'S FANTASTIC

ARE YOU TRYING TO HOOK UP WITH ME?
NO...
THIS IS A FACT FINDING MISSION.
FACT:
SEX IS GOOD.

WII WII

YOU EVER WONDER WHAT YOU'D DO IF YOU WERE INVOLVED IN A FARMING ACCIDENT?
WHY WOULD I BE FARMING?
I'M JUST SAYING, WHAT WOULD HAPPEN IF ALL YOUR LIMBS WERE CHOPPED OFF BY A TRACTOR?
PROBABLY SPEND A LOT MORE TIME ON THE INTERNET.
HOW WOULD YOU TYPE?
WITH MY PENIS, I GUESS.
THOUGH IT'D BE HARD, WITH THE GIRTH I POSSESS.
BE A LOT OF KEY MASHING, LET ME TELL YOU.
YOU SHOULD STAY AWAY FROM FARMS.
IF YOU EVER GET AN E-MAIL THAT SAYS 'WERTSDFGXCVB', YOU'LL KNOW IT'S FROM ME.

BUT WE'RE DOING IT ANYHOW

WHAT ARE YOU DOING?
I THOUGHT WE WOULD HAVE SEX NOW.
SEX?
THIS IS FOREPLAY!
TROJAN
BOOT
REJECTED!

INSTANT GRATIFICATION IS BETTER WITH A PLAN

I DEMAND GELATO!
THAT'S FINE, BUT THERE WAS AN ACCIDENT THIS MORNING AND THE ROADS ARE ALL BLOCKED UP.
THE UNIVERSITY OF CHICAGO SCAVENGER HUNT ROAD TRIP
WE'LL NEED TO WALK.
ROADS?
WHERE WE'RE GOING, WE DON'T NEED ANY ROADS.
YOU HAVE WAY TOO MUCH DISPOSABLE INCOME.
AFTER MY FROZEN ITALIAN SNACK, I'M GOING BACK IN TIME TO HAND YOUR FATHER A CONDOM.

MOM RULEZ

SPENT MOTHER'S DAY WITH MY PARENTS YESTERDAY, AND MY MOM THOUGHT IT WOULD BE FUN TO RELIVE PART OF MY YOUTH BY MAKING MY LUNCH FOR TODAY.
CUTE.
Have a good day of work, honey.
Oh, and please don't get thrown into jail in an attempt to be cellmates with Paris Hilton.
She probably won't be in the mood to do you, or let you tape it.
WANT TO COME WITH ME TO BEST BUY TO RETURN A VIDEO CAMERA?
WE CAN BUY YOU THOSE GILMORE GIRLS DVDS YOU'VE BEEN EYEING.
AND MAYBE A BRA.

FORWARD THINKING

HI THERE, I'M–
LET ME STOP YOU RIGHT THERE.
GIVEN THE AMOUNT OF WOMEN THAT I MEET ON A DAILY BASIS, LEARNING NAMES IS COMPLETELY INEFFICIENT.
INSTEAD, I'D LIKE YOU TO JOIN A NEW PILOT PROGRAM I'M FUNDING AND DEVELOPING,
PATENT PENDING.
FROM HERE ON IN, YOU WILL BE REFERRED TO AS GIRL #458392.
MY COLLEAGUE HERE WILL JUST MAKE YOUR DESIGNATION SLIGHTLY MORE PERMANENT.
BITE DOWN ON THIS, MISS.

DUCK SOUP DU JOUR

GOOD EVENING, GUYS.
HI.
I'M RAYNE, AND THIS IS MY BUDDY, DUCKY.
DUCKY?
THAT'S WHAT IT SAYS ON HIS BIRTH CERTIFICATE.
THEY REALLY NAMED YOU 'DUCKY'?
HE WAS RAISED BY DUCKS.
SO, WHAT CAN I GET YOU?
PITCHER OF BEER, PLEASE.
I'M GOING TO HAVE THE FAJITAS, AND DUCKY WILL HAVE SOME STALE BREAD BROKEN UP INTO LITTLE PIECES SOAKED IN POND WATER.

I GO, JUGO, WE ALL GO

HOW DO YOU KNOW IF YOU'RE IN LOVE?
IF YOU CAN PICTURE HER POOPING AND STILL WANT TO HAVE SEX AFTERWARDS, YOU'RE THERE.
THAT WAS STRANGELY DEEP AND DISGUSTING AT THE SAME TIME.
BALANCE. YIN AND YANG, BABY.
EVEN APPLIES TO POOP.

HAPPINESS IS A WARM PEANUTS

PSYCHIATRIC HELP 5¢
THE DOCTOR IS IN
PSYCHIATRIC HELP 5¢
CLINK
THE DOCTOR IS IN
PSYCHIATRIC HELP 5¢
IT BURNS WHEN I PEE.
PSYCHIATRIC HELP 5¢

FLIPPING THE BIRD

COO COO
COO COO
COO COO
COO
COO
COO COO
COO
COO COO
COO
COO
COO COO
COO
COO COO
THEY'RE ORGANIZING.
THAT'S THE ONLY EXPLANATION.
OBVIOUSLY.
IT HAS NOTHING TO DO WITH THE CASES OF MELTING CRÈME EGGS IN YOUR TRUNK.

IF YOU CAN MAKE IT THERE...

RAYNE, I NEED A SMALL FAVOR.
WHAT'S IT THIS TIME?
IF YOU WANT ME TO FIX THE OZONE LAYER, I'LL NEED AT LEAST TWO WEEKS AND A GIANT STYROFOAM HAMMER.
I'D LIKE YOU TO GO TO NEW YORK CITY-
NYC?
NY MEEEEEEEEEEEEEEEEEE!
DO YOU THINK THAT'S A 'YES'?
THE @$$HOLE HAS LEFT THE BUILDING.

UP, UP AND AWAY

WHP WHP WHP WHP WHP
IT'S A HELICOPTER.
WHAT IS THAT?
IT'S LIKE A PLANE WITH NO WINGS.
WHERE ARE YOU GOING?
NEW YORK CITY,
AND YOU'RE BOTH COMING WITH.
I'LL DROP THE ROPE LADDER DOWN AND WE'LL GO.
WHY DON'T YOU JUST LAND, AND WE'LL GET ON BOARD THAT WAY?
ROPE.
LADDER.

JAZZ HANDS!

CAN'T WAIT TO DO SOME SHOPPING-
WELL, AT LEAST WE CAN HIT UP A FEW CLUBS-
YOU GOT US TICKETS FOR EVERY MUSICAL IN NEW YORK CITY, DIDN'T YOU?
YOU ARE THE GAYEST STRAIGHTEST MAN I HAVE EVER KNOWN.
IF I GO THROUGH YOUR SUITCASE, WILL I FIND A PAIR OF CROTCHLESS LEATHER PANTS?

GNARLY

DO WE HAVE A DEAL?
WE DO AT THAT.
SO?
IT WAS A TOUGH NEGOTIATION, BUT WE'RE ONLY GOING TO SEE ONE SHOW AND YOU GET TO DO YOUR SHOPPING.
YEAH, HI THERE,
I'M GOING TO NEED TWENTY PIZZAS, SIX CASES OF ANCHOVIES AND A FEW OF THOSE ILLEGAL BEAR TRAPS PETA ARE ALWAYS HARPING ABOUT.
AND IN RETURN?
WE HAVE TO HELP HIM SET TRAPS AROUND THE CITY FOR TEENAGE MUTANT NINJA TURTLES.
WE ALSO MAY NEED THREE PAIRS OF NUNCHUKS FOR MY FRIENDS AND I IF THINGS GET OUT OF HAND.

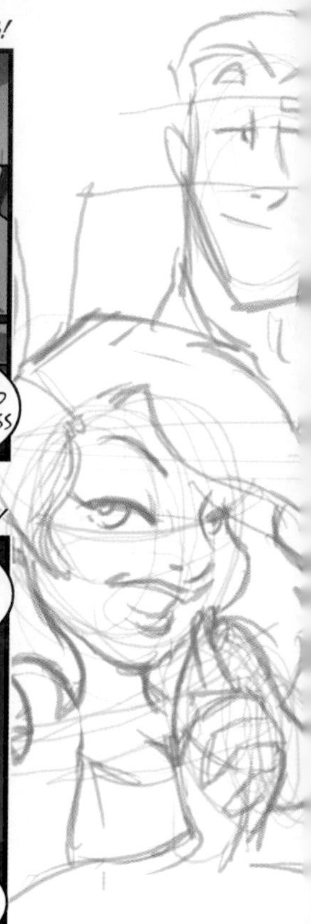

ROAD RAGING

THE AMOUNT OF TRAFFIC IN THIS CITY IS RIDICULOUS.
YOU'VE GOT TO BE A GUANO EATING INSANE PERSON TO OWN OR OPERATE A CAR HERE.
SINCE LEAVING THE AIRPORT, WE'VE BEEN STUCK IN THE CAR FOR THREE DAMN HOURS.
I CAN'T TAKE IT.
AAAAAAAAH!!
MUST BE NICE TO HAVE A FREAK OUT WHEN YOUR COMPANY IS PAYING FOR EVERYTHING.
QUICK! NO TIME!
TAKE OFF ALL YOUR CLOTHES AND GET IN!

SIZE 360 PANTIES

THINGS TO DO IN NEW YORK
Violate the Statue of Liberty
I THINK YOU MEAN 'VISIT'
DON'T THINK I DO, NO.

NANTS INGONYAMA!
FROM THE DAY, WE ARRIVE ON THE PLANET
THEY ALMOST LOOK LIKE REAL ANIMALS.
OF COURSE.
BAGITHI BABA
DID YOU REALLY HAVE TO RIDE THE PERFORMERS?
EXIT
IT'S A TESTAMENT TO THEIR CRAFT THAT I EVEN WANTED TO!
COME ON, BABE
WHY DON'T WE PAINT THE TOWN?
AND ALL THAT JAZZ
I'M GONNA ROUGE MY KNEES
AND ROLL MY STOCKINGS DOWN
PLAYBILL
CHICAGO
AND ALL THAT JAZZ.
OH COME ON NOW!
LA CAGE AUX FOOLS
YOU'RE OUT OF CONTROL.
EXIT
MY NAME IS RAYNE, AND I LIKE TO RIDE PEOPLE.
HELLO, RAYNE.

'C' IS FOR-

I'LL GIVE YOU ONE MORE CHANCE TO SEE A SHOW AND THEN THAT'S IT.
WHAT DO YOU WANT TO SEE?
I'VE HEARD GOOD THINGS ABOUT AVENUE Q.
WHAT'S IT ABOUT?
PUPPETS-
I'M NOT SEEING A SHOW WITH PUPPETS-
-DIRTY ONES THAT HAVE SEX.
SEATS IN THE FRONT ROW WOULD BE GREAT, PLEASE.
Avenu
Q
he Music
MY FRIEND HERE WOULD JUST LOVE TO GET A FACE SHOT WITH SOME FELT SEMEN.

EYE OF THE TREKKIE

I HATE TO SAY IT,
BUT THESE PERFORMERS HAVE SOME TALENT.
RMISSION
MUSICAL THEATRE JUST MAY BE PUT ON THE LIST OF 'THINGS RAYNE CAN'T DO'.
OUT OF CURIOSITY, HOW LARGE IS THAT LIST?
WITH THIS NEW ENTRY...
THREE.
IN ALL THE WORLD, THERE ARE ONLY THREE THINGS YOU CAN'T DO?
WHAT'S NUMBER TWO?
SKIPPING ROPE.
YOU CAN'T SKIP ROPE?
WHO AM I? ROCKY?

YOU CAN'T PUT YOUR FINGER THERE!

WHAT DID YOU THINK?
DID YOU SEE THE PART WHERE THE PUPPETS 69'ED EACH OTHER?
I THINK HE LIKED IT.
COME ON, LET'S GO GRAB A LATE DINNER-
WAIT.
WHEN ARE WE GOING TO HANG OUT WITH THE CAST?
WHAT DO YOU MEAN?
THE GIRL WITH THE KATE MONSTER PUPPET WAS RATHER HOT, AND IT WOULD BE A SHAME TO NOT SEE WHAT WOULD RESULT IN OUR COMBINED TALENTS.
YOU'RE GOING TO CHASE A WOMAN WHO SPENDS MOST OF HER TIME WITH HER HAND UP A PUPPET'S ASS?
REMINDS ME OF THE TIME HE WENT AFTER THE PROCTOLOGIST.
SHE EXPLORED AREAS OF MY BODY THAT I REGRET.

LIVE AT THE IMPROV

HELLO.
I JUST WANTED TO SAY THAT I'M A HUGE FAN...
...MARY FABER.
SMOOTH.

MOVING RIGHT ALONG

YOU TWO READY?
FOR WHAT?
Avenu
WE WERE INVITED TO HANG OUT WITH THE CAST AND CREW OF AVENUE Q AT A PUB A FEW BLOCKS DOWN.
HOW'D YOU PULL THAT ONE OFF?
nue
I SPOKE TO MARY IN A LANGUAGE I KNEW SHE'D UNDERSTAND.
NOW KISS MY PUPPET, AND LET'S GO.
Ave

YOU CAN TAKE THE GUYS OUT OF THE PARK BUT...

MY BUDDY'S MOM BROKE HER HIP LAST WEEK.
WHAT'S WITH OLD WOMEN AND BREAKING THEIR HIPS?
THERE SOME TYPE OF CLUB YOU GET TO JOIN AFTERWARDS?
IT SUCKS.
IT USED TO BE OUR GRANDPARENTS, NOW ITS OUR PARENTS.
IT'S SCARY.
YOU KNOW THERE'S GOING TO COME A DAY WHERE I PUSH YOU DOWN SOME STAIRS, BREAK YOUR HIP, AND CALL YOU AN OLD WOMAN, RIGHT?
PRESUMABLY.
IS THIS REALLY WHAT YOU GUYS TALK ABOUT WHEN YOU'RE ALONE?

I SEE YOU BROUGHT YOUR WORK HOME WITH YOU.
I'VE GOTTEN SORTA ATTACHED TO KATE MONSTER AND THE PROP GUYS WERE FEELING GENEROUS.
PUPPETRY OF THE...
I'LL JUST PUT HER AWAY-
NO-NO,
LET THE PUPPET STAY.
YEAH, SO I THINK I JUST HAD A THREESOME INVOLVING A PUPPET.
GLAD YOU'RE ENJOYING YOUR WORK TRIP.
IN ADDITION TO LEARNING ABOUT INANIMATE OBJECT INTERCOURSE, SEEING AVENUE Q HAS INSPIRED ME EVEN FURTHER.
YOU'RE OPENING A MUPPET BROTHEL?
I'VE DECIDED TO CREATE MY VERY OWN PUPPET-FEATURING BROADWAY SHOW.
STARRING P DOT,
THE MILITANT SCOTSMAN.
OVERTURE!
OI!
YOU'RE IN THE FRONT ROW.
THAT'LL BE $350 A PIECE.

THE PRODUCERS

EXCUSE US.
MMM?
I'M JEFF AND THIS IS BOBBY.
WE'RE THE CREATORS OF AVENUE Q.
I'M RAYNE, CREATOR OF BILLIONS OF SPERMATOZOA
THE CREATIVE PROCESS IS MAGICAL, ISN'T IT, BOYS?
GOOD TALK.

THE INTERNET IS FOR WEBCOMICS

WE DON'T APPRECIATE YOU HITTING ON ONE OUR PERFORMERS.
SHOULD'VE CAST ROSIE O'DONNELL THEN.
I HEAR SHE'S NOT DOING ANYTHING.

P DOT HAS SOMETHING TO SAY.

YOU BROUGHT THIS UPON YOURSELF
THIS JUST GOT SURREAL.

THEY COULD BREAK INTO SONG AT ANY MOMENT.

NOT IN YOUR HANDS

M&M'S WORLD
WHAT DO YOU WANT TO DO NEXT-
THE TIME FOR REVOLUTION IS NOW.
CADBURY EGGS FOREVER!
BOOT!

TYPECASTING

FEEL LIKE STOPPING IN AT THE FOX BUILDING?
I REFUSE TO ACKNOWLEDGE THEM UNTIL THEY GREEN LIGHT MY TV MOVIE.
YOUR WHAT NOW?
I PITCHED THEM A MOVIE CONCEPT A WHILE BACK.
A CONCEPT SO BOLD AND PROVOCATIVE THAT IT WILL BRING IN MORE VIEWERS THAN ALL THE AMERICAN IDOLS COMBINED.
AWESOME
THE RAYNE SUMMERS STORY
BASED ON TRUE EVENTS.
YOU START CASTING YET?
YEAH, BUT NOTHING'S SET IN STONE.
I'M THINKING ANDY DICK OR THAT KID WHO PLAYED URKEL FOR YOU.

THAT SUPERMAN THING

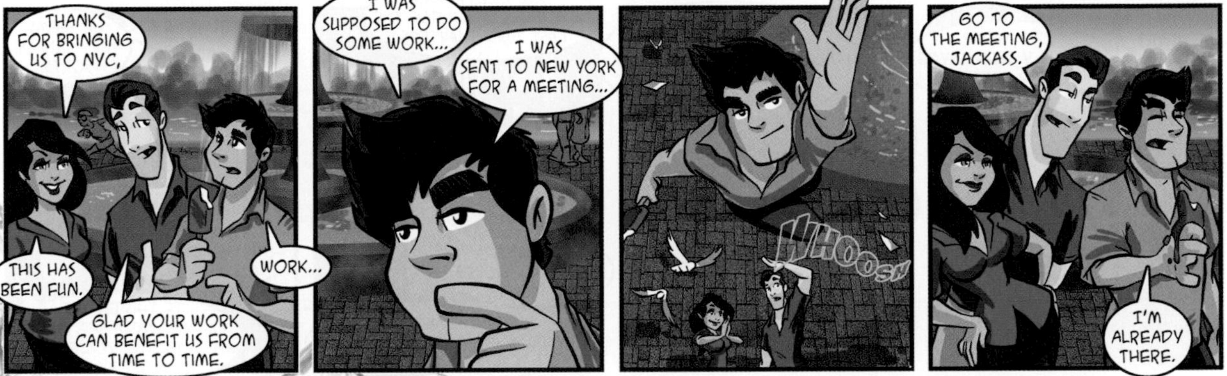
THANKS FOR BRINGING US TO NYC,
THIS HAS BEEN FUN.
GLAD YOUR WORK CAN BENEFIT US FROM TIME TO TIME.
WORK...
I WAS SUPPOSED TO DO SOME WORK...
I WAS SENT TO NEW YORK FOR A MEETING...
WHOOSH
GO TO THE MEETING, JACKASS.
I'M ALREADY THERE.

NO.

GOOD AFTERNOON.
I'M HERE TO MAKE A STATEMENT.
FROM HERE ON IN, WE WILL ALL ONLY BE WEARING PANTS WHEN ABSOLUTELY NECESSARY, AS STATED IN THE CHARTER OF THE AMERICAN PANTS ASSOCIATION.
TODAY, WE CELEBRATE OUR INDEPENDENCE...
FROM PANTS!
YOU HAVE NO IDEA WHY YOU'RE HERE.
I THOUGHT THAT WAS PAINFULLY CLEAR.

AN HONORABLE MAN

WHY ARE WE HERE?
I'VE NEVER ACTUALLY SEEN RAYNE AT WORK BEFORE.
I THOUGHT IT WOULD BE FUN SEEING HIM OUTCLASSED BY THE REAL PROFESSIONALS AND OUT OF HIS ELEMENT.
YOUR SALES FIGURES HAVE BEEN DOWN FOR THE LAST TWO QUARTERS.
THE NUMBERS ARE EITHER GOING TO PICK UP,
OR THE UNEMPLOYMENT RATE IS GOING TO GO UP JUST A TINY BIT THIS YEAR.
OH YES.
HE SEEMS VERY OUT OF SORTS.
I WAS AT LEAST HOPING FOR A RIDICULOUS METAPHOR.
IF THIS ENTIRE OFFICE WAS A SHIP, AND I WAS A PIRATE, YOU'D ALL BE PILLAGED BY NOW.

BOSSA NOVA!

KLANK
KLANK
KLANK
NO TURTLES?
NOTHING MUTANT OR NINJA AT ALL DOWN THERE.
WE HAVE BEEN MISINFORMED, MY FRIEND,
GREATLY MISINFORMED.

VOICE OF THE TIMES

OUR OBSESSION WITH CELEBRITY IS UNHEALTHY,
IT'S TRUE, AND NEEDS TO BE SAID
BUT I'D STILL LIKE TO TALK ABOUT A GIRL ANYWAY,
A GIRL OF WHOM I SAW GIVE HEAD
SHE DROVE WITHOUT PERMISSION,
AND SHE DROVE LOADED WITH BOOZE
WE ALL WATCHED IT CLEARLY,
IN WHAT CNN CALLS 'THE NEWS'
BUT THERE'S NO POINT IN KEEPING PARIS IN JAIL,
SHOULD THEY REALLY EVEN TRY?
I VOTE WE BRING BACK THE ELECTRIC CHAIR,
AND LET THE BITCH FRY!

YOU SHOULD SEE THE SECRET HANDSHAKE

EXCUSE ME, MISS?
YES?
BY THE AUTHORITY INVESTED IN ME, BY THE AMERICAN PANTS ASSOCIATION, I MUST INSIST THAT YOU REMOVE YOUR PANTS IMMEDIATELY AND WITHDRAW FROM THE PREMISES.
WITH ME.
I WOULD THINK YOUR STUPID PANTS ASSOCIATION JOKE WOULD BE OLD BY NOW.
HOW MUCH DO I OWE IN DUES THIS YEAR?
EIGHTY-FOUR DOLLARS.

NUMBER THREE

THE TAO OF RAYNE
PREPARE TO BE AMAZED.
THE SIZE, TEXTURE AND AMOUNT OF YOUR POOP IS ONLY IMPRESSIVE TO YOU.

DOUBLE DOG DARE

IM IN UR COMIX

AFTERNOON, LITTLE SISTER.
HOW'D YOU GET THIS NUMBER?
I GOT MY OWN CAT TODAY.
FOLLOWING IN MY FOOT STEPS?
I'VE HAD BABY FOR YEARS.
I NAMED HIM QUI-GON JINN, JEDI MASTER.
THAT'S A STUPID NAME.
I'M THINKING ABOUT INJECTING MY CAT WITH MIDI-CHLORIANS.
DIDN'T ASK.

BA WEEP GRANNA WEEP NINNY BANG

HEY GOD,
IT'S ME, RAYNE.
LISTEN, I KNOW YOU'RE PROBABLY NOT TOO FOND OF ME, SEEING AS HOW I DON'T BELIEVE IN YOU
AND TEND TO USE YOUR TEN COMMANDMENTS AS A CHECKLIST OF THINGS TO ACCOMPLISH IN MY LIFETIME
BUT I NEED YOU NOW.
PLEASE, **PLEASE** LET THE TRANSFORMERS MOVIE BE GOOD AND DON'T ALLOW MICHAEL BAY TO RAPE OUR COLLECTIVE CHILDHOODS.
'TIL ALL ARE ONE.
'TIL ALL ARE ONE.

I'M DOING MY PART TOO!

WHERE YOU GOING?
OUT.
YOU KNOW THAT SCENE, IN STARSHIP TROOPERS, WHERE THE BUGS SUCK OUT THE SOLDIER'S BRAIN TO LEARN WHAT HE KNOWS?
I'M GOING OUT WITH KATE.
DAMN.

POOR MILTON

KATE, KATE, KATE...
NAME DOESN'T RING A BELL, H-UH?
NO-NO,
I KNOW EXACTLY WHO THAT IS.
THAT'S THE ONE...
WHO CAME HERE FROM FAR OFF..
TO ...PROTECT...
US ...
FROM THE DECEPTICONS...
SOMETIMES SHE TRANSFORMS... INTO A TRUCK?
YES, I'M GOING OUT THIS EVENING WITH OPTIMUS PRIME.
THE TOASTER IS GOING TO BE DEVASTATED.

DON'T TOUCH THE NUTS

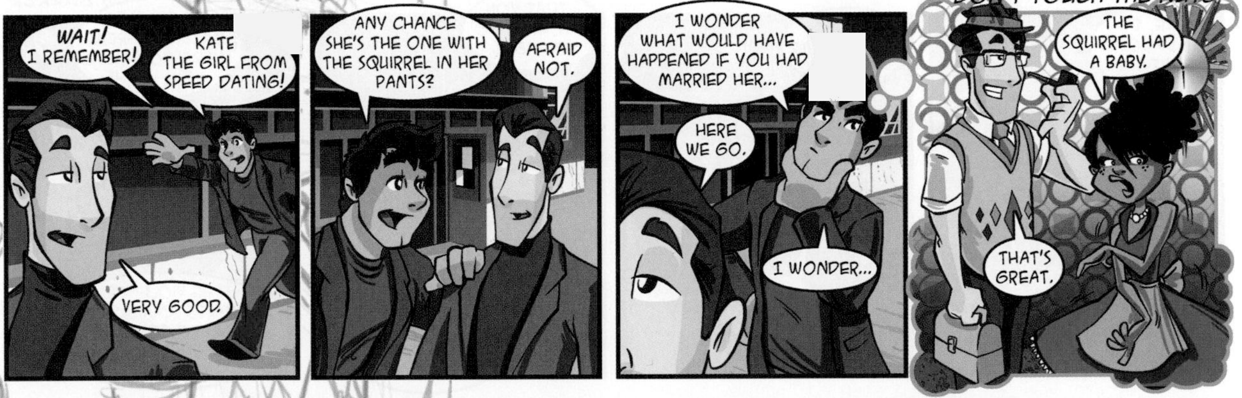

WHO'S ON FIRST IMPRESSIONS

THANK YOU BOB BARKER

KATE, I'M REALLY SORRY ABOUT THIS.
HE JUST FOLLOWED ME HERE.
HE'S LIKE A PUPPY...
...THAT YOU JUST WANT TO STRANGLE.
AND THEN NEUTER TO PROTECT FUTURE GENERATIONS.
SO I'M NOT MAKING A GREAT IMPRESSION RIGHT NOW, H-UH?
THE VIOLENCE TOWARDS ANIMALS ISN'T IN THE PRO COLUMN, BUT I THINK THE SMILE MAKES UP FOR IT.

MENTOS DISABILITY

I'VE HAD A REALLY GOOD TIME TONIGHT.
ME TOO.
SO..?
SO...
DO YOU WANT TO...COME BACK TO MY PLACE?
COULD BE FUN.
THANK YOU, ROOFIE COLADA!
I THINK IT'S TOO SOON FOR THAT JOKE.
YEAH,
I'M NOT USUALLY THE ONE WHO MAKES THE PUNCH LINES.
SORRY.

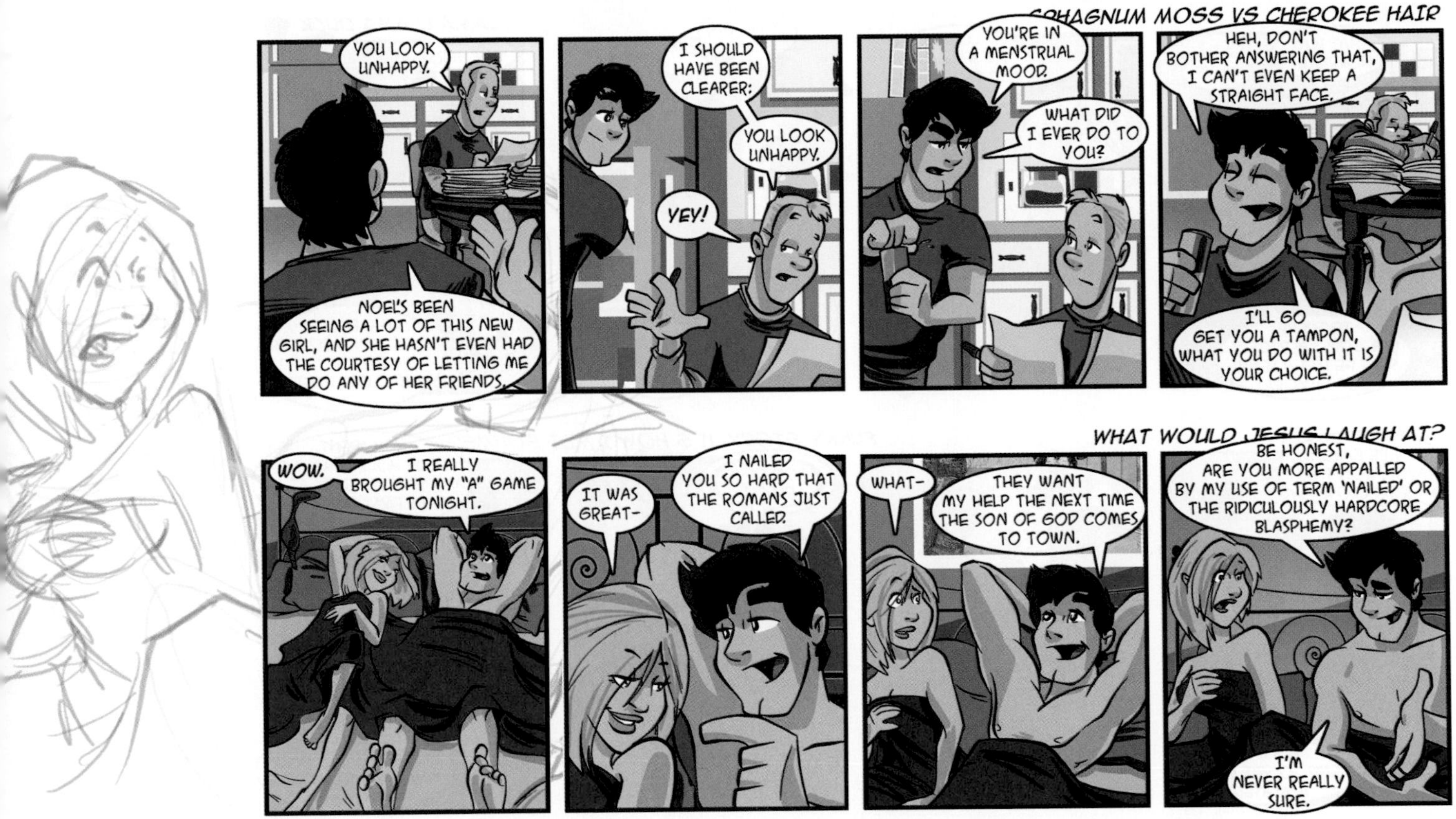
SPHAGNUM MOSS VS CHEROKEE HAIR
YOU LOOK UNHAPPY.
NOEL'S BEEN SEEING A LOT OF THIS NEW GIRL, AND SHE HASN'T EVEN HAD THE COURTESY OF LETTING ME DO ANY OF HER FRIENDS.
I SHOULD HAVE BEEN CLEARER:
YOU LOOK UNHAPPY.
YEY!
YOU'RE IN A MENSTRUAL MOOD.
WHAT DID I EVER DO TO YOU?
HEH, DON'T BOTHER ANSWERING THAT, I CAN'T EVEN KEEP A STRAIGHT FACE.
I'LL GO GET YOU A TAMPON, WHAT YOU DO WITH IT IS YOUR CHOICE.
WHAT WOULD JESUS LAUGH AT?
WOW.
I REALLY BROUGHT MY "A" GAME TONIGHT.
IT WAS GREAT-
I NAILED YOU SO HARD THAT THE ROMANS JUST CALLED.
WHAT-
THEY WANT MY HELP THE NEXT TIME THE SON OF GOD COMES TO TOWN.
BE HONEST, ARE YOU MORE APPALLED BY MY USE OF TERM 'NAILED' OR THE RIDICULOUSLY HARDCORE BLASPHEMY?
I'M NEVER REALLY SURE.

LLAMA LLAMA DUCK

THAT WAS HORRIBLE!
WHY?
IF THERE IS A GOD, I'M PRETTY SURE HE HAS A SENSE OF HUMOR.
LOOK AT A LLAMA, AND TELL ME HE DOESN'T.
COME ON, DUDE.
NO-NO, I WASN'T TALKING ABOUT **YOU**.
I MEANT THE OTHER LLAMA.
WAY HARSH.
HOW MANY LLAMAS DO YOU HAVE, EXACTLY?
THE BETTER QUESTION WOULD BE, HOW DO THEY OPEN AND CLOSE DOORS?

FUNNY STORY: IT'S HOW I MET SOHMER

NOW BE CAREFUL, RAYNE, DON'T GET TOO CLOSE.
LLAMAS TEND TO SPIT WHEN AGITATED.
PBBBT!!!
SON OF A **BITCH**.
YOU SPENT FOUR HOURS CHASING AND SPITTING BACK AT ME THAT FIRST DAY, DUDE
TO THIS DAY, IT REMAINS THE ONLY TIME I'VE CONDONED SPITTING.

THE GLASS IS HALF FULL

DID YOU HEAR ABOUT YOUR FRIENDS OVER AT CADBURY BEING TAKEN TO COURT FOR HEALTH CODE VIOLATIONS?
APPARENTLY THERE WERE SOME DRAINAGE PIPE ISSUES OVER THE CONVEYORS.
H-UH.
THEY ALSO PLEAD GUILTY TO THREE OFFENCES REGARDING SALMONELLA.
SO WHAT YOU'RE SAYING IS THAT THERE'S LIKELY TO BE A BLOWOUT SALE ON CADBURY EGGS IN THE NEAR FUTURE?
ENJOY THE STOMACH PUMPING.
IN OR OUT, THEY'RE STILL MAGICALLY DELICIOUS.

LET SPECULATION REIGN!

WHAT'S THAT?
A LETTER FROM THE MANAGEMENT.
THE MANAGEMENT?
THE ARTIST AND THE WRITER.
THEY LIKE TO FEEL IMPORTANT BY GIVING THEMSELVES FANCY TITLES.
JACKASSES.
WERE YOU GOING TO READ IT?
ON MONDAY.
FOR NOW, I THOUGHT I WOULD TAKE ADVANTAGE OF THINGS WHILE THE LINES OF COMMUNICATION ARE OPEN.
DEAR JACKASSES,
PLEASE MAKE ISSA'S CHARACTER EASIER-
HEY.
-AND DEAF.

THAT SQUIGGLE SAYS 'SOHMER'

Blind Ferr
ENTERTAINMENT
To the cast of LICD,
We have decided that from this moment, the clock will start for all of you
You will no longer be 24 forever, and instead will age normally, like your creators and your readers.
You will evolve, you will grow old.
AND NOW A REBUTTAL:

I WISH.

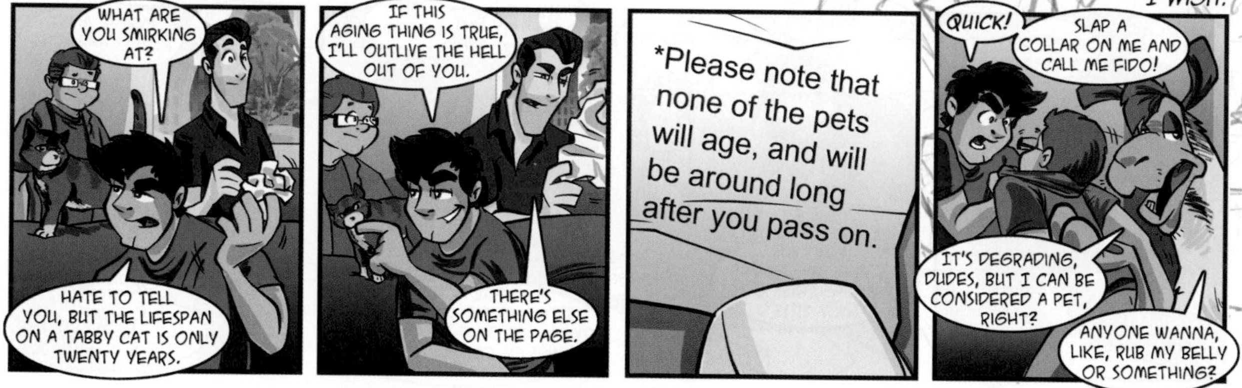
WHAT ARE YOU SMIRKING AT?
HATE TO TELL YOU, BUT THE LIFESPAN ON A TABBY CAT IS ONLY TWENTY YEARS.
IF THIS AGING THING IS TRUE, I'LL OUTLIVE THE HELL OUT OF YOU.
THERE'S SOMETHING ELSE ON THE PAGE.
*Please note that none of the pets will age, and will be around long after you pass on.
QUICK!
SLAP A COLLAR ON ME AND CALL ME FIDO!
IT'S DEGRADING, DUDES, BUT I CAN BE CONSIDERED A PET, RIGHT?
ANYONE WANNA, LIKE, RUB MY BELLY OR SOMETHING?

DOUBLE TEQUILA AND RED BULL

10:47:25 AM
10:47:27 AM
10:47:28 AM
YEAH, I CAN'T JUST SIT HERE WAITING TO DIE.
WHO'S UP FOR A LITTLE MASS SUICIDE?
I'LL GET THE PUNCH.
10:47:29 AM

IOA KNOW

YOU KNOW WHAT?
FORGET THIS.
I'M NOT GOING TO LIVE MY LIFE ACCORDING TO SOMEONE ELSE'S RULES.
I'M WITTY, HILARIOUS, GORGEOUS AND POSSESS A SUPERIOR INTELLECT.
GUSTAV KLIMT
I'LL FIND MYSELF A NEW HOME WHERE THEY APPRECIATE ME.
AND WHERE YOU DON'T AGE?
AND WHERE I DON'T BLOODY AGE.
WHERE ARE YOU GOING TO GO EXACTLY?
I HAVE A FEW THOUGHTS.
GET FUZZY

WITH ALL RESPECT TO LYNN JOHNSTON

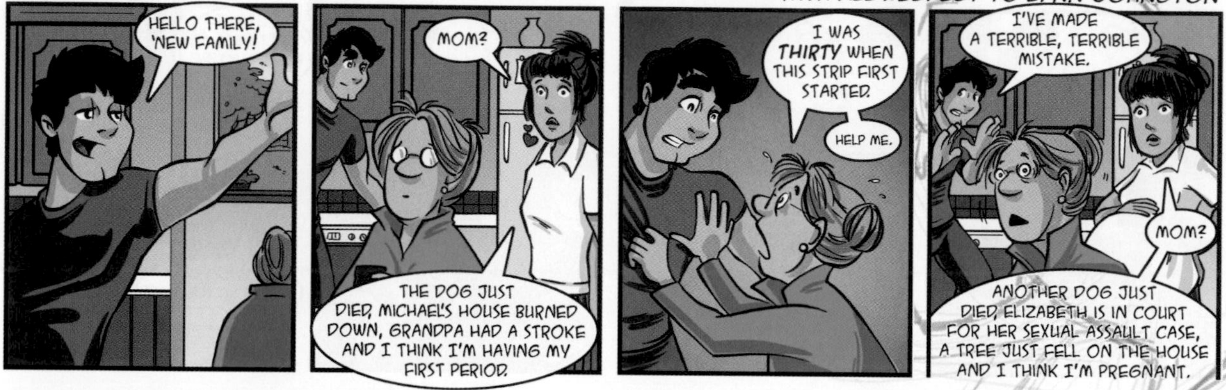
HELLO THERE, 'NEW FAMILY!
MOM?
THE DOG JUST DIED, MICHAEL'S HOUSE BURNED DOWN, GRANDPA HAD A STROKE AND I THINK I'M HAVING MY FIRST PERIOD.
I WAS THIRTY WHEN THIS STRIP FIRST STARTED.
HELP ME.
I'VE MADE A TERRIBLE, TERRIBLE MISTAKE.
MOM?
ANOTHER DOG JUST DIED, ELIZABETH IS IN COURT FOR HER SEXUAL ASSAULT CASE, A TREE JUST FELL ON THE HOUSE AND I THINK I'M PREGNANT.

HER BREASTS WILL ALWAYS BE PERFECT

OKAY.
YOU WIN.
I'LL AGE.
UNLESS THE DEVIL-
NO.
FINE.
BUT DON'T COME CRYING TO ME WHEN YOUR BREASTS ARE AT YOUR KNEES,
MICK IS FATTER THAN ROSIE,
NOEL LOSES HIS HOUSE IN THE DIVORCE
AND JOHN FALLS DOWN A WELL.
I DON'T THINK LIFE'S GOING TO BE ALL THAT BAD.
YOU'RE BAD!
YEAH.
I WENT THERE.

WE SHALL

I JUST BOUGHT MYSELF A CONDO, BUT WITH HOW THINGS WORKED OUT WITH MY OLD PLACE, I NEED TO MOVE IN TODAY.
I NEED YOUR HELP TO GET IT DONE.
I CALLED YOUR WORK AND TOLD THEM YOU WEREN'T COMING IN THIS MORNING BECAUSE YOU WERE IN SCOTLAND HUNTING NESSIE WITH A FLASHLIGHT, AN AXE AND YOUR INGENUITY.
IN ADDITION, WE'RE RENTING A 28 FOOT TRUCK WHICH YOU'LL BE DRIVING, EQUIPPED WITH YOUR VERY OWN CONSTRUCTION HELMET.
AND OF COURSE, THE RED BULL'S WAITING FOR YOU IN THE CAR,
WITH THREE DIFFERENT TYPES OF STRAWS.
SHALL WE?

VATICAN CITY STATE, 00120

TRUCK-TRUCK-TRUCK, I GET TO DRIVE A TRUCK.
TRUCK-TRUCK-

WHAT IS IT?
A LOT OF VERY PLEASANT WORDS END IN 'UCK'.
THAT CAN'T BE RANDOM.
I THINK THAT MAY BE PART OF 'INTELLIGENT DESIGN'.
YOU SHOULD WRITE A LETTER TO THE CATHOLIC CHURCH.
I'LL MAIL IT.

AIRMILES?

YES, I'LL TAKE THE FULL INSURANCE PACKAGE PLEASE.
NO DEDUCTIBLE.

GOOD TO GO

BAM
CRASH
SCREEEEEEEEE
MY BAD.
HE...
HE JUST...
NO DEDUCTIBLE.

HE WHO HESITATES

WHAT MADE YOU DECIDE TO MOVE?
FIGURED IT WAS TIME I STOPPED WASTING MONEY ON RENT.
SO I FOUND THIS NEW GREAT PLACE IN MY PRICE RANGE,
AND MY LANDLORD WAS KIND ENOUGH TO LET ME OUT OF MY OLD LEASE.
YEAH, YOUR MOM'S A NICE LADY.
LEFT AT THE LIGHT?
YOU JUST GOING TO KEEP IGNORING THAT, THEN?
IF MICK DIDN'T WANT TO RIDE IN THE BACK, HE SHOULD HAVE BEEN QUICKER WHEN I LOCKED HIM IN.

MALICE AFORETHOUGHT

TAPES $CDS
UP
FROM THE LIVING ROOM, I'M TAKING MY TV AND THE GLASS COFFEE TABLE.
THE SIDE TABLES TOO.
THE GOOD NEWS IS THAT WE'RE ONLY MOVING TWO APPLIANCES-
YOU HAVE A BAT.
ANYWAY YOU LOOK AT IT, YOUR STUFF IS GETTING BUSTED UP TODAY.
I'M JUST TRYING TO BE EFFICIENT ABOUT IT.

MIRACLES OF MODERN SCIENCE

ME!
(CUTE CHICK)
YAY! GENIUS!
(YOU)
YOU WANT TO TOSS MY WASHING MACHINE OUT OF THE WINDOW?
THAT IS PART OF THE OVERALL PROCESS TO ACHIEVE THE DESIRED GOAL, YES.
MAYBE INSTEAD OF THAT PLAN, YOU COULD ACTUALLY LIFT SOMETHING-
I'M ALREADY FINISHED PRODUCTION ON THE TINY PARACHUTES.
THEY HAVEN'T BEEN FULLY TESTED, BUT MY R+D DEPARTMENT IS VERY CONFIDENT THAT THEY'LL PERFORM ADEQUATELY.
IT'S TRUE. WE ARE.

ONE SMALL STEP FOR OTTOMANKIND

CAPCOM?
WE ARE A 'GO'.
GUIDANCE?
GO.
AND WE ARE A GO FOR PROPULSION.
CRASH
THE COUCH HAS LANDED!
GOOD JOB EVERYONE, BUT LET'S NOT GET AHEAD OF OURSELVES.
BRING THE GLASS COFFEE TABLE TO THE DECK AND PREPARE FOR ANOTHER LAUNCH.

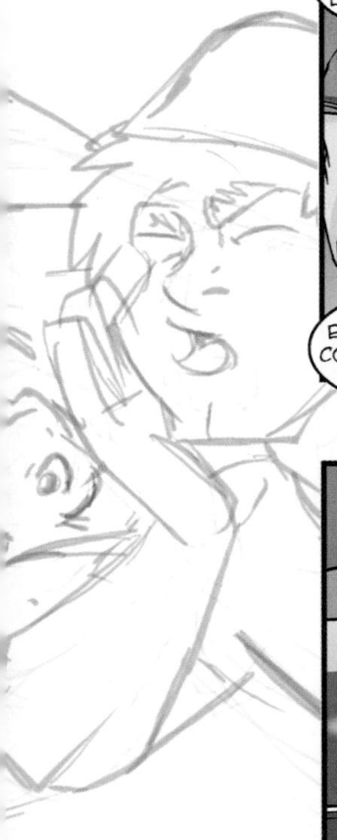

WOWZERS!

ARE YOU EVEN LIFTING?
NO, I JUST THOUGHT I WOULD STAND HERE AND SWEAT OUT OF MY KNEE CAPS FOR FUN.
I DIDN'T EVEN KNOW YOU COULD SWEAT OUT OF KNEE CAPS.
LIFT HIGHER.
I'M GOING AS HIGH AS I BLOODY CAN.
YOU CAN GO HIGHER!
YOU'RE RIGHT. I APOLOGIZE.
GO-GO GADGET ARMS!
I'M NEVER ASKING YOU TO HELP ME MOVE AGAIN.
HEAVENS NO!
TODAY TRULY IS THE DAY THE MUSIC DIED.

HEY, GOOD BUDDY

MEEP.
TAP
TAP
TAP
AOOOOOOOOOGA!

UCK OFF
YOU WENT THROUGH A RED LIGHT.
WHAT'S A COP GOING TO DO?
I'M IN A TRUCK.
HE'S LUCKY I DIDN'T BRAKE SUDDENLY.
YOU JUST CUT OFF THAT SMART CAR.
I'M IN A TRUCK.
YOU-
I'M IN A TRUCK.
THERE'S NOTHING I CAN'T DO.
PARALLEL PARK.
TOUCH.
IT'S PRONOUNCED 'TOO-SHAY'.
I'M. IN. A. TRUCK.
BYE, BUH-BYE, BYE, GOOD BYE...
BAM
SCREEECH
YOU EVER WONDER WHAT INCIDENT THE RENTAL INSURANCE WON'T COVER?
AND I'M NOW GOING TO ENSURE THAT MY SEAT BELT IS BUCKLED SECURELY AND SAY A LITTLE PRAYER TO WHATEVER DEITY WILL LISTEN.

THE MASTER OF BETA

WHEN WE GET THERE, WE GET TO TAKE EVERYTHING OFF THE TRUCK AND PUT IT INTO THE NEW PLACE.
IF THAT WAS THE ULTIMATE PLAN, WOULDN'T IT HAVE MADE MORE SENSE TO NOT HAVE MOVED ANYTHING AT ALL IN THE FIRST PLACE?
I'M SO TIRED.
DON'T WANT TO MOVE ANYMORE.
THEN HOW-
I'M RAYNE SUMMERS.
GOD'S MIRACLE CHILD.
I ALWAYS HAVE A **PLAN B.**
THE ACTUAL PLAN, NOT THE PHARMACEUTICAL PRODUCT.
I FIGURED THAT, YEAH.

IF IT'S NAY SCOTTISH, IT'S CRAP!

NANCY,
IT'S RAYNE.
GET ME THE FOREIGN MINISTER OF NEPAL, THE PILOT OF OUR CORPORATE JET AND WHATEVER LOCAL OFFICIAL HANDLES IMMIGRATION.
YEAH, NESSIE IS DOING JUST FINE.
AND THANKS FOR ASKING.

HE NEEDS A BIGGER BOX

THIS IS THE BOX.
THIS IS WHERE I THINK.
YOU'LL NOTICE THAT IT IS, IN FACT, OUTSIDE THE BOX.
YOU HIRED SHERPAS.
I HIRED SHERPAS.

MISSING LINK

YOU KNOW WHAT'S FUNNY ABOUT NEPAL?
THEIR CURRENCY IS THE 'RUPEE.'
WHY IS THAT FUNNY?
THAT'S THE SAME CURRENCY THEY USE IN THE ZELDA GAMES!
FASCINATING.
AND HE'S GONE.
HAI!
<Tourist.>
<Let's wait until he falls asleep then take his shield.>

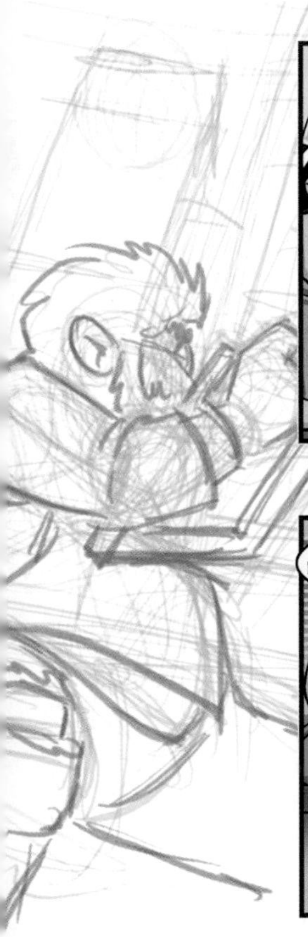

IN A FAMILY WAY

THAT'S THE LAST ONE.
SIGN HERE.
IT'S BEEN A LONG DAY, BUT IT LOOKS LIKE WE'RE DONE.
AND HERE.
THANKS-
WHAT HAVE I BEEN SIGNING?
IMMIGRATION PAPERS FOR THE SHERPAS.
INCIDENTALLY, THEY'RE GOING TO NEED SOME PLACE TO STAY UNTIL THEY CAN FIND LEGAL EMPLOYMENT.
PAPA?

HE DOESN'T EVEN DRINK SCOTCH

WELCOME BACK TO WORK.
ENJOY YOUR DAY OFF?
BEFORE YOU START WITH THE SARCASM, I HAVE PROOF THAT I WAS IN FACT DOING WHAT I STATED.
I PRESENT TO YOU AN ARTIST'S RENDITION OF MY ADVENTURE IN SCOTLAND.
I SAW YOUR HOMELESS FRIEND DRAW IT JUST A MINUTE AGO THROUGH THE WINDOW.
HE'S NESSIE?
WEAK.
YOUR CALL LIST IS ON YOUR DESK.

MAYOR OF A SMALL VILLAGE

YOU KNOW WHAT TERM I'VE RECENTLY COME TO ENJOY?
DO TELL.
EXECUTIVE PRIVILEGE.
USE IT IN A SENTENCE.
YOU JUST DEFLOWERED MY 18 YEAR OLD SISTER!
HOW COULD YOU DO THAT?
EXECUTIVE PRIVILEGE.
THAT MUST COME IN HANDY.
THE WONDERS OF ELECTED OFFICE, MY FRIEND, LET ME TELL YOU.

AND ALL THAT JAZZ

ARE YOU EVER GOING TO APOLOGIZE, BY THE WAY?
YOU TALKING ABOUT...

MR MICHAEL BAY, SIR, IF YOU'RE READING, I'D LIKE TO APOLOGIZE FOR ASSUMING THAT YOU'D CREATE A HORRIBLE TRANSFORMERS MOVIE.
YOU MADE A FUN POPCORN FILM,
AND INSTEAD OF RAPING OUR COLLECTIVE CHILDHOODS, YOU ONLY REACHED INTO OUR CHILDHOODS' PANTS POCKET AND RUBBED UP AGAINST ITS JUNK A BIT.
I CAN LIVE WITH THAT.
CLOSE ENOUGH.

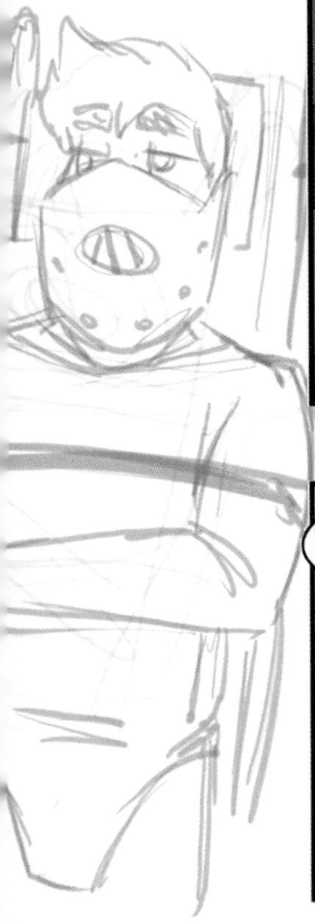

BAGDASARIAN ASPIRATIONS

HI.
WHAT'S UP?
HEY.
HE LEARNED ABOUT THE CGI ALVIN AND THE CHIPMUNKS MOVIE THAT'S COMING UP?
YEP.
I'M A DANGER TO THOSE AROUND ME.
CAN YOU CRUMBLE UP A COOKIE AND PUT IT IN MY MOUTH?

WOOD FOR SHEEP

LISTEN BUDDY, I DON'T WANT TO PUT ANY PRESSURE ON YOU BUT...
HA!
OUR TWO NATIONS ARE STILL AT WAR!

TACO FLAVORED KEESES

I HAVE A WEDDING THIS WEEKEND
I DON'T THINK IT'S STILL CONSIDERED WEDDING WHEN THE SECOND PARTY IS AN INANIMATE OBJECT, PAL.
UNLESS IT'S A TV, THEN GO WITH GOD.
WHOSE WEDDING IS IT?
NOT SURE YOU EVER MET,
SHE'S AN OLD FRIEND FROM SCHOOL AND WORK,
VICTORIA STEELE.
IS SHE AWARE SHE HAS A PORN STAR NAME?
ANY CHANCE THE GUY SHE'S MARRYING IS NAMED 'ROCK SEXINGTON'?
NO.
IF THEY HAVE A KID, THEY SHOULD NAME IT 'HUMP'.
WORKS FOR BOY OR GIRL!
I'LL PASS THAT ALONG WITH THE WEDDING GIFT.

WHERE'S BUCKY?

RAYNE, CAN YOU-
I'M THE NEW CAPTAIN AMERICA.
SLAM
IS MR. SUMMERS-
HE'S OUT.
TELL ALL YOUR FRIENDS.

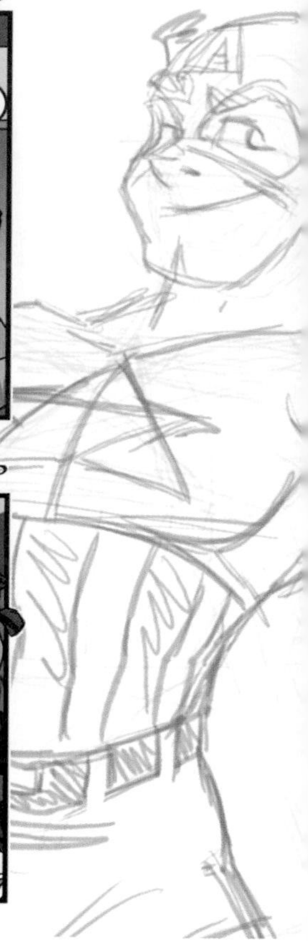

THE SOURCE OF HIS POWER

YOU KNOW WHAT?
I AM GETTING SICK AND TIRED OF THESE MORONIC SELF HELP AUTHORS FILLING THE GULLIBLE MASSES WITH THE CONCEPT OF ACHIEVEMENT BY WISHING.
AND PLEASE DON'T THINK I'M AIMING THIS TIRADE AT 'THE SECRET,'
I HAVE NOTHING BUT GOOD THINGS TO SAY ABOUT IT.
IT IS A WONDERFUL BLUDGEONING TOOL.
LISTEN, NOTHING IN LIFE IS GIVEN TO YOU BY THE ACT OF SITTING ON YOUR ASS AND THINKING PRETTY THOUGHTS.
YOU WANT SOMETHING IN LIFE?
THEN YOU GO AND TAKE IT.
YOU TOOK OFF MY BRA WHILE I WAS NAPPING.
I WANTED IT.

EVERY DAY IS CUTE-URDAY

60,000 B.C.
1,000 AD
PRESENT DAY
EVOLUTION IS A CRUEL AND UNFORGIVING MISTRESS.
BUT SHE KNOWS CUTE,
I'LL GIVE HER THAT.

HMMMMM....

YOU'RE AWFULLY CLOSE.
YEAH, I WASN'T SO MUCH EXPECTING YOU TO STOP LIKE THAT.
ALSO, YOU SMELL LIKE BACON.
I LIKE THAT.
WE JUST WENT OUT FOR BREAKFAST.
I'VE GOT TO GO, I'LL CATCH YOU LATER.
YOU'RE NOT INVITING ME UPSTAIRS?
NOW'S NOT THE BEST TIME.
I SEE.

DEFCON DELTA AGAIN

CODE GREY! CODE GREY!
AND I HAVE NO IDEA WHAT THAT MEANS.
BUT THANKS FOR THE VISIT.
IT MEANS NOEL'S BEEN ACTING WEIRD, AND WE ARE OBLIGATED TO FIND OUT WHY.
WISH I COULD, BUT I HAVE TO GET THESE PROMOS DONE TODAY.
CODE PINK! CODE PINK!
THAT ONE MEANS I'M GAY?
THAT ONE MEANS YOU'RE GAY AND SUBMISSIVE.

THOSE CODES WRITE THEMSELVES

CODE ORANGE! CODE ORANGE!
FINE.
Orange Julius
THAT'LL BE $3.95 PLEASE.
CODE GREEN! CODE GREEN!
THAT'S NOT GETTING OLD AT ALL.

THE OTHER HALF IS VIOLENCE

WHAT DO YOU THINK WE SHOULD DO?
HONESTLY?
NOTHING.
I HAVEN'T NOTICED ANYTHING OUT OF THE ORDINARY.
THEN AGAIN, YOU SPEND MORE TIME WITH HIM THAN I DO.
THAT SAID, WHY DON'T WE JUST RING THE DOORBELL AND ASK NOEL WHAT'S GOING ON?
WHUMPF
I APPRECIATE YOUR INPUT, BUT I'M GOING TO GO WITH MY INSTINCTS HERE.
NOW CAN I GET A 'YO JOE!' PLEASE?
YO JOE.

HAPPY LITTLE TREES

DADDY!
WHAT'S THE MATTER, JEFF?
DADDY! SNAKE EYES WAS OUTSIDE MY WINDOW
AND HE SAID BAD WORDS.
IT WAS JUST A DREAM.
GO BACK TO BED, PAL.
BUT DADDY!
MAYBE YOU SHOULD GO TAKE A LOOK AT HIS ROOM TO MAKE SURE?
THAT'S CRAZY.
EVERYONE KNOWS SNAKE EYES CAN'T TALK.
AFTER I'M DONE HAULING YOUR CHIP FILLED ASS UP THIS WALL, I'M TAKING YOU BACK TO THE GYM.
I WANT TO MAKE A COMEBACK, I REALLY DO,
BUT ALL I CAN FOCUS ON IS THAT YOU PROBABLY BOUGHT THAT GRAPPLING HOOK FROM WAL-MART.

SHERLOCK HOLMES ON HOMES

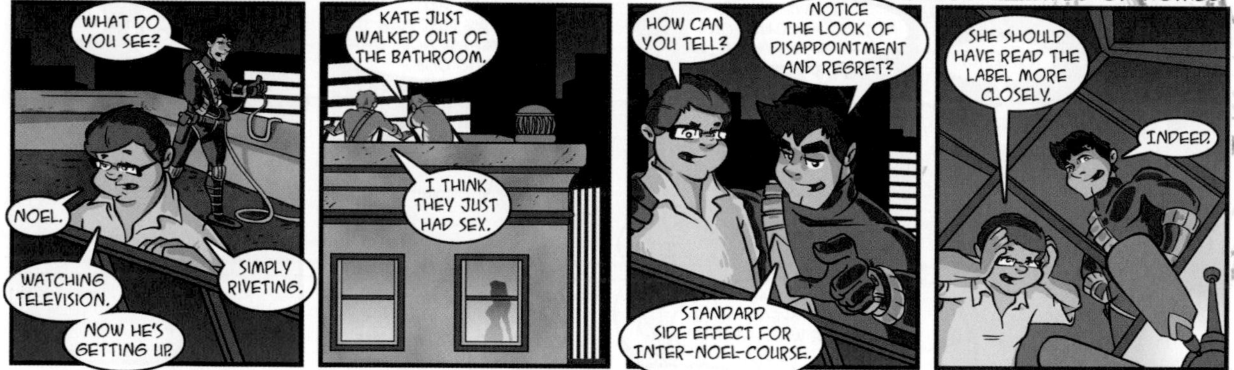

WHAT DO YOU SEE?
NOEL.
WATCHING TELEVISION.
SIMPLY RIVETING.
NOW HE'S GETTING UP.
KATE JUST WALKED OUT OF THE BATHROOM.
I THINK THEY JUST HAD SEX.
HOW CAN YOU TELL?
NOTICE THE LOOK OF DISAPPOINTMENT AND REGRET?
STANDARD SIDE EFFECT FOR INTER-NOEL-COURSE.
SHE SHOULD HAVE READ THE LABEL MORE CLOSELY.
INDEED.

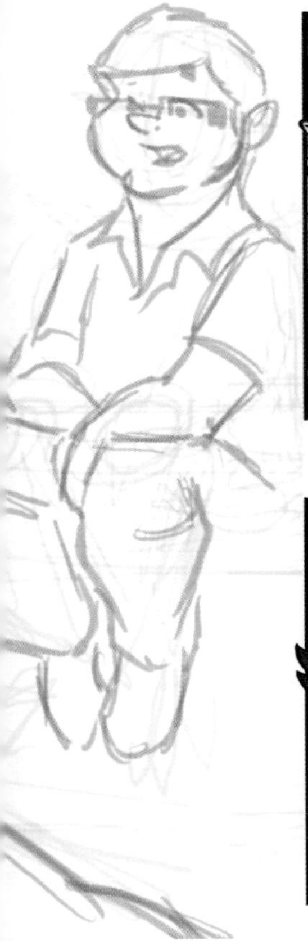

A VERY FRIENDLY NEIGHBOURHOOD

THINKING ABOUT ROBBING THE PLACE?
LITTLE BIT, BUT YOU'D PROVIDE COMPLICATIONS.
FOR EXAMPLE, OUR GETAWAY WOULD CONSIST OF YOU TAKING THREE STEPS, RUNNING OUT OF BREATH, PASSING OUT AND WAITING FOR THE COPS TO CARRY YOU TO A SQUAD CAR.

I'D SWING TO SAFETY FROM BUILDING TO BUILDING WITH MY WEB SHOOTER.
WHEN I WOKE UP AT THE STATION, I'D NARC YOU OUT.
THAT'S WHY **YOU'LL** NEVER BE SPIDERMAN!

EVERYONE LOVES A SURPRISE

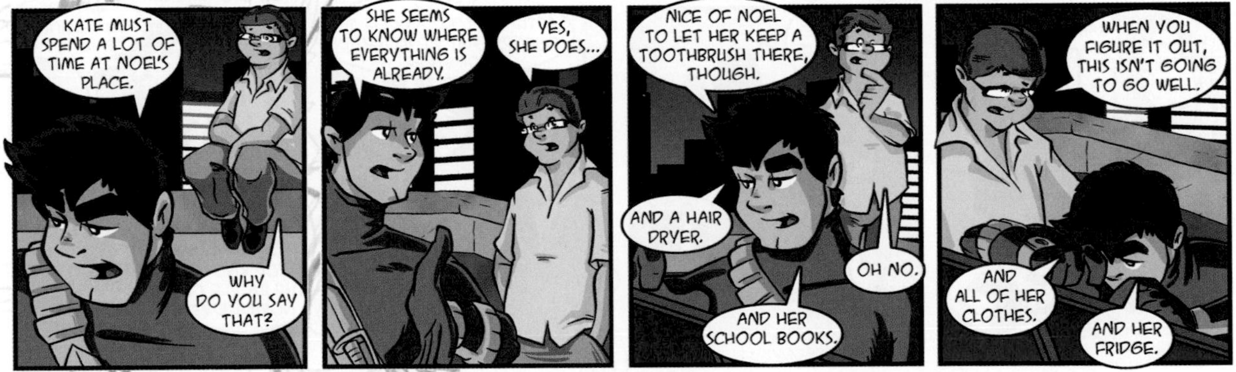

KATE MUST SPEND A LOT OF TIME AT NOEL'S PLACE.
WHY DO YOU SAY THAT?
SHE SEEMS TO KNOW WHERE EVERYTHING IS ALREADY.
YES, SHE DOES...
NICE OF NOEL TO LET HER KEEP A TOOTHBRUSH THERE, THOUGH.
AND A HAIR DRYER.
AND HER SCHOOL BOOKS.
OH NO.
WHEN YOU FIGURE IT OUT, THIS ISN'T GOING TO GO WELL.
AND ALL OF HER CLOTHES.
AND HER FRIDGE.

INTERCESSION

KNOCK KNOCK
HEY, WHAT'S UP?

LIFE'S A BEACH

BABY?
MMMM?
THERE'S SOMETHING YOU OUGHT TO KNOW.
THAT WOULD BE?
I NEVER ACTUALLY TOLD ANY OF MY FRIENDS THAT WE MOVED IN TOGETHER.
I FIGURED AS MUCH.
WHY ARE YOU TELLING ME THIS NOW?
YOU KNOW THE BATTLE OF NORMANDY?
OUR CONDO IS ABOUT TO PLAY THE PART OF 'THE BEACH!

STOP!

FUNNY THING ABOUT IMPULSE SHOPPING IS THAT YOU USUALLY DON'T KNOW HOW WORTHWHILE YOUR PURCHASE IS GOING TO BE.
YOU TRY TO LISTEN TO OTHER PEOPLE,
THOUGH IT REALLY IS YOUR OWN CALL.
THE SALES GUY SAID I WAS CRAZY TO PURCHASE SUCH A BIG HAMMER,
BUT I JUST KNEW.
AND HERE WE ARE.
THIS ISN'T A RENTAL!
THIS ISN'T A RENTAL!

GREEN THUMB UP THE BUTT

AND NOT JUST BECAUSE OF THE PLANT IN MY ASS.
I KNOW THAT TOO.

REASONABLE RATES

BEFORE WE DELVE DEEP INTO THE CRAPPINESS THAT IS NOEL,
IS THERE ANY CHANCE THAT I HAVE MISUNDERSTOOD THIS SITUATION?
PERHAPS KATE HERE IS JUST YOUR LIVE-IN CLEANING LADY THAT YOU GET TO BANG FOR A NOMINAL FEE?
THAT PAUSE IS GOING TO COST ME.
SEE IF SHE CAN COME BY MY PLACE ON TUESDAYS.

WHAT WOULD MATLOCK DO?

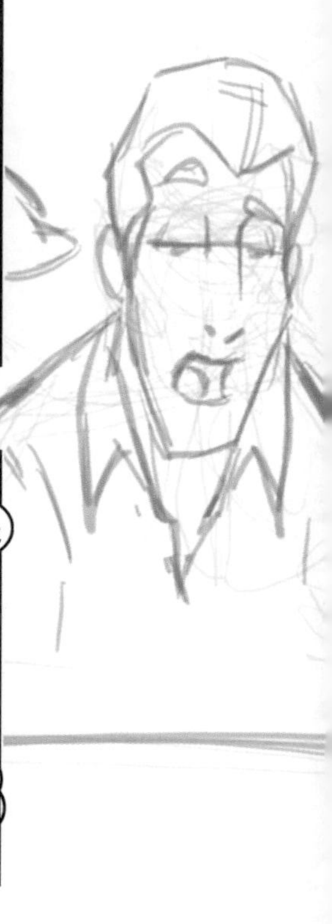

ONE SHALL STAND

I'M SORRY FOR NOT TELLING YOU ABOUT KATE AND ME.
I JUST DIDN'T KNOW HOW YOU'D REACT TO IT.
YOU'RE NOT SO GOOD WITH THIS TYPE OF THING.
AND WHAT TYPE OF THING MIGHT THAT BE?
CHANGE.
I'M GREAT WITH CHANGE!
I LOVE CHANGE!
I THINK IT'S THE NEATEST.
I WISH I COULD CHANGE RIGHT NOW INTO A CAR AND RUN YOU OVER.
CHANGE TO HIM IS BEING A TRANSFORMER.
ROLL OUT!

BF 4 EVA

I'M SORRY FOR NOT BEING UP FRONT WITH YOU. I MESSED UP.
I KNOW IT'S SOON, BUT I LOVE KATE A GREAT DEAL AND IT FELT RIGHT.
SO WE MOVED IN TOGETHER.
I UNDERSTAND.
I WISH YOU BOTH NOTHING BUT HAPPINESS.
AND MAY I ASK THE MORE PRESSING QUESTION?
HOW WILL ALL THIS AFFECT **YOU?**
HOW WILL ALL THIS AFFECT **ME.**
YOU WANT A HUG, DON'T YOU?
MAYBE.
THAT'S MY CUE FOR BED.
BE SURE TO WAKE ME WHEN YOUR TESTOSTERONE RETURNS.

CALLED TO THE BARS

SO WHAT'S MY PUNISHMENT FOR THIS TRANSGRESSION?
I THINK YOU ALREADY KNOW.
TZAANG!
SCHZING!
THE GOOD NEWS IS THAT MY COSTUME GUY JUST GOT HIS LAW DEGREE.
HE EARNED IT NIGHTS AND WEEKENDS, SO YOU KNOW HE'S GOING TO BE EXTRA GOOD.

BLOWOUT SALE

MICK IS GETTING SEX ON A REGULAR BASIS.
WITH A FEMALE.
A HUMAN FEMALE.
NOEL FELL IN LOVE AND IS NOW LIVING WITH...
THAT GIRL...
WITH THE NAME.
EVERYTHING'S CHANGING.
I DON'T KNOW HOW MUCH MORE OF THIS I CAN TAKE.
SUCK FOR $1.50
NEW 2007 PRICING!

FINGER LICKIN' GOOD

WHAT'S THE MATTER WITH YOU?
I THINK I HAVE TO GROW UP.
BE AN ADULT AND STUFF.
WILL YOU BE MY GIRLFRIEND?
I'M MARRIED AND I HAVE A CHILD.
IS THAT A NO?
I'M AFRAID SO.
ARE YOU A LESBIAN?
I'M GOING TO GO EAT NOW.
A SNACK?
A LADY SNACK?

PREPARE FOR GLORY

WHY AM I GETTING THE UNDENIABLE URGE TO GET INTO A RELATIONSHIP LIKE MY FRIENDS?
IS THAT REALLY THE BEST COURSE FOR ME?
HELP ME.
I AM LOST IN A SEA OF UNCERTAINTY.
UNCA, YOU SAID WE WERE GOING TO WATCH 300 TODAY.
I'M NOT PAYING YOU FOUR BUTTONS AN HOUR TO WATCH MOVIES!
WHICH REMINDS ME,
YOU HAVE AN OUTSTANDING BALANCE OF 24 BUTTONS-
LET'S GO WATCH THE MOVIE.

FOSSI BEAR

TWO BIG THINGS TO TELL YOU.
SURE.
FIRSTLY, I NOW HAVE A GIRLFRIEND.
WE'RE IN LOVE.
AND SUCH.
AND THE SECOND THING?
I WILL NOW PUNCTUATE ALL IMPORTANT DECLARATIONS LIKE THIS:
JAZZ HANDS!

NOW I'VE GOT THAT JINGLE STUCK IN MY HEAD

YOU HAVE A GIRLFRIEND.
YES.
GOING TO TELL ME ABOUT HER?
OF COURSE.
MOSTLY, SHE WALKS DOWN STAIRS...
ALONE OR IN PAIRS...
AND MAKES A SLINKITY SOUND.
YOU'RE DOING THE SLINKY SONG.
SHE'S A MARVELOUS THING.
ALSO, VERY SPRINGY.

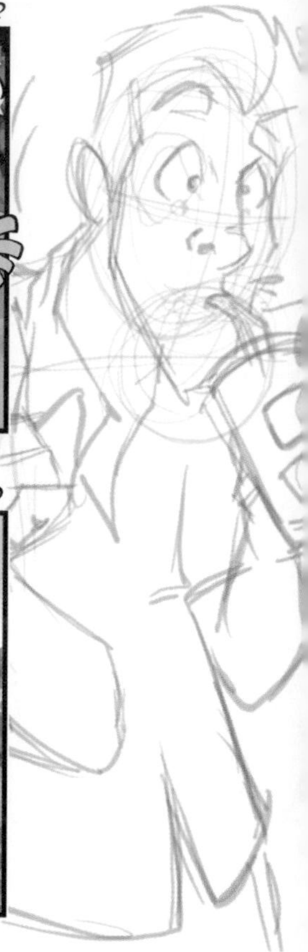

COMEDY GOLD, BABY!

KATE AND I ARE GOING OUT WITH MICK AND HIS GIRLFRIEND TONIGHT.
WHY DON'T YOU AND SLINKY JOIN US?
WE'D BE DELIGHTED.
THANK YOU.
THIS WHOLE SETUP IS REEKING OF TELEVISION SITCOM CHEESE.
I WAS THINKING THE SAME THING.
GOINK!
CLIK
HA HA HA HA HA HA HA HA HA HA HA HA

FOR FUN SHE'S A WONDERFUL TOY!

I'LL TAKE THAT ONE, PLEASE.
UNLESS YOU HAVE A SIMILAR VERSION WITH LARGER BREASTS?
SIR, I'M GOING TO NEED TO SEE YOUR OLYMPIC COMMITTEE CREDENTIALS, PLEASE.
WELL, I'M GOING TO NEED TO SEE PROOF THAT THIS GIRL IS OVER EIGHTEEN.
CHECKMATE.

RELATIONSHIPS FOR DUMMIES

FORGOT YOUR GIRLFRIEND IN THE CAR, DIDN'T YOU?
APPARENTLY.
YOU PLANNING ON GOING TO GET HER?
NOT SURE.
WHAT'S THE STANDARD COURSE OF ACTION FOR SOMETHING LIKE THIS?
YOU. GO. AND. GET. HER.
REALLY?
GO AND GET HER!
THIS RELATIONSHIP STUFF IS PRETTY WILD.

WHEN FIGS PLY

EVERYONE, THIS IS SLINKY.
YOU CAN CALL ME SELINE.
IT'S NICE TO MEET YOU.
SHE IS MY GIRLFRIEND.
IS THAT ON THE MENU?
WE'LL FIND OUT, SWEETHEART.

A FRIEND INDEED

SHE LOOKS AWFULLY YOUNG.
HOW CAN YOU TELL?
THEN AGAIN,
IF YOU CAN TELL A TREE'S AGE BY COUNTING ITS RINGS...
I GUESS I NEED TO SEE HER VA-
I TOOK THAT JOKE IN A VERY MISGUIDED DIRECTION.
RAYNE!
DO SOMETHING DISTRACTING!
I'M ON IT.
GOINK!
SPLASH

GET BUSTED

SO HOW DID YOU GUYS MEET?
I'M A PROFESSIONAL GYMNAST,
AND RAYNE WAS OVER AT OUR GYM WHILE SCOUTING FOR THE OLYMPICS.
AFTER MY ROUTINE, RAYNE WAS THERE WITH A TOWEL AND A BOTTLE OF WATER.
I JUST KNEW.
I AM AWFULLY CONSIDERATE.
I DIDN'T KNOW YOU WERE PART OF THE OLYMPIC COMMITTEE.
THERE'S A LOT ABOUT ME YOU DON'T KNOW.
WHEN ARE YOU PLANNING ON TELLING HER YOU'RE BATMAN?
I'M IN NO RUSH.
GOING TO TAKE IT SLOW.

BASICS

HOW HAVE THINGS BEEN GOING WITH SELINE THE LAST COUPLE OF WEEKS?
IT'S BEEN A LEARNING EXPERIENCE.
CARE TO PASS ON YOUR NEWFOUND WISDOM?
MY PLEASURE.
FOR EXAMPLE, IF YOUR GIRLFRIEND SLEEPS OVER, A PROPER GOOD MORNING DOES NOT INCLUDE THE WORDS:
"OH, YOU'RE STILL HERE?"
AND WHAT HAPPENED WITH THE WHOLE CUDDLING ISSUE?
I STILL DON'T SEE THE POINT IN TOUCHING IF I'M NOT GOING TO EJACULATE, BUT WHAT'RE YOU GOING TO DO?
THE WOMEN. THEY LIKES IT.

THE DRINK OF ASTRONAUTS

I LOVE YOU.
I ALSO LOVE JUICE.
ONE DAY, YEARS FROM NOW, YOU'RE GOING TO LOOK BACK AT THIS MOMENT AND FEEL REALLY BAD THAT YOU DIDN'T LAUGH.

I LOVE THIS GUY

SHE TOLD YOU SHE LOVED YOU, AND THAT'S HOW YOU REACTED?
OH, IT GETS BETTER.
I'M MORTIFIED.
I CAN'T BELIEVE I TOLD YOU-
I LOVE-
WHY IS THIS HAPPENING TO ME?
MAYBE IF YOU HAD JESUS IN YOUR HEART, THINGS LIKE THIS WOULDN'T HAPPEN.
WOW.
I KNOW.
I REALLY RAISED THE BAR FOR MEN EVERYWHERE, H-UH?

BUT HE'S IN JEOPARDY!

WHAT DID YOU END UP DOING?
I MATURELY EXPLAINED THAT WHILE I HAD GREAT FONDNESS HER, I DID NOT FEEL THE SAME WAY.
WHAT DID YOU REALLY END UP DOING?
WHAT ANY OTHER MALE WOULD HAVE DONE.
YOU PANICKED AND JUST TOLD HER WHAT SHE WANTED TO HEAR.
YOUR EYES ARE AWFULLY ACCUSING RIGHT NOW.
I LOVE YOU TOO?
IT SHOULDN'T BE IN THE FORM OF A QUESTION.

WHERE YOU GOING?
AS MUCH AS YOU MAKING ME FEEL WORSE IS GREAT AND ALL,
I HAVE ANOTHER APPOINTMENT.
TO DO WHAT?
WORK STUFF.
WE'RE TRYING TO WIN A GOVERNMENT CONTRACT FOR A HIGHLY ADVANCED WEAPON SYSTEM.
AND RAYNE WILL FORM...
THE HEAD!
BACK TO PLANET DOOM
WE'RE STILL IN THE CONCEPTUAL PHASE.
LET ME ASK YOU A QUESTION.
OH BOY.
DO YOU THINK LOIS WAS ANGRY AT CLARK?
PARDON?
YOU KNOW,
DO YOU THINK SHE WAS PISSED OFF AT HIM FOR KEEPING HIS WHOLE 'I AM SUPERMAN' THING TO HIMSELF, AND LYING TO HER ABOUT IT?
KNEEL BEFORE ZOD!
YOU'RE NOT GOING TO GET ME TO SAY THAT IT'S OKAY TO LIE TO YOUR GIRLFRIEND.
SO YOU WOULD'VE BEEN HAPPY IF LEX LUTHOR HAD KILLED LOIS TO GET TO SUPERMAN?
REAL NICE.

FIRST TIME CALLER

WHAT DO I DO?
STOP TELLING HER THAT YOU LOVE HER, FOR ONE.
OTHER THAN THAT, WHY NOT JUST SEE WHAT HAPPENS?
SHE'S A NICE GIRL, FUN TO HANG OUT WITH,
SEXES ME UP WHENEVER I SO CHOOSE,
REALLY SMOOTH SKIN-
MOVE ALONG.
THIS IS GOING TO SOUND A BIT ODD COMING FROM ME, BUT SHE'S...

IMMATURE...
YOU HAVE A GI JOE LUNCH BOX.
IT IS A SCIENTIFIC FACT THAT STORM SHADOW MAKES LUNCH 17% MORE DELICIOUS.
I WILL NOT BE DENIED THAT FLAVOR ON ACCOUNT OF PERCEPTION!

OUR DOMAIN IS SHADOW

SO THE WEATHER...
YEAH...
IT'S THERE.
YEP.
WEATHER.
LADIES, I'M SORRY,
BUT THIS ISN'T WORKING.
HAVING THE TWO OF YOU WITH US ON OUR WALK JUST ISN'T NATURAL.
WE ARE GIANT NINJA.
THIS ISN'T NATURAL EITHER.

I DON'T KNOW EITHER

I WAS THINKING...
NAKED TIME IS NOT THINKY TIME.
THAT'S PRACTICALLY A LAW.
ANYHOW, I WAS THINKING THAT MAYBE IT'S TIME TO MEET YOUR PARENTS.
GOOD. GOOD.
IS IT OKAY IF I ASK HER 'WHY'?
NEIN!

HE WENT THERE

NOW SHE WANTS TO MEET MY PARENTS!
WHAT THE HELL IS HAPPENING HERE?
YOU NEVER KNOW. YOU MIGHT SOON GET HIT WITH 'WHERE IS THIS GOING? MY BIOLOGICAL CLOCK IS TICKING'
YOU HAVE A WITTY RETORT ALREADY PLANNED, DON'T YOU?
GO AHEAD.
I'LL BE ALL LIKE:
"TAKE OUT THE DAMN BATTERY!"
SNAP
BE SURE TO GET HER REACTION ON VIDEO.
WE COULD PROBABLY BEAT THE FAT JEDI KID IN VIEWS.

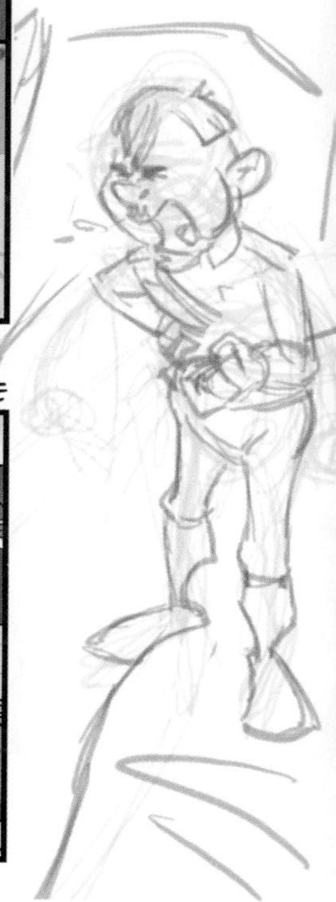

OH SHE'S OFFENDED, ALL RIGHT

ARE YOU GOING TO BRING SELINE TO MEET YOUR PARENTS?
HELL NO,
I'D RATHER NOT GIVE MY MOTHER FALSE HOPES.
I DID THAT ONCE BEFORE...
HI HONEY-
OH, WHO'S THIS?
A GIRLFRIEND?
MAYBE WHEN YOUR FATHER GETS HOME, THE FOUR OF US CAN HAVE DINNER TOGETHER-
RAYNE?
WHY IS SHE BLIND-FOLDED?
I DIDN'T WANT HER TO KNOW WHERE WE LIVED.
IT'S COOL THOUGH,
I TOLD HER YOU WERE BLIND AND THAT PEOPLE WITH SIGHT OFFEND YOU.

LEGAL POT USER

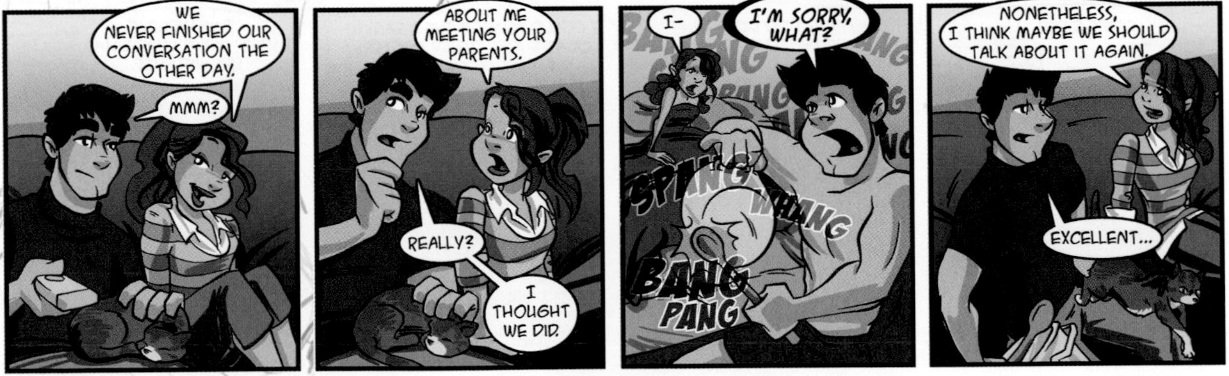
WE NEVER FINISHED OUR CONVERSATION THE OTHER DAY.
MMM?
ABOUT ME MEETING YOUR PARENTS.
REALLY?
I THOUGHT WE DID.
I-
I'M SORRY, WHAT?
SPANG
WHANG
BANG
PANG
NONETHELESS, I THINK MAYBE WE SHOULD TALK ABOUT IT AGAIN.
EXCELLENT...

COS-FOREPLAY

MONDAY
TUESDAY
WEDNESDAY
THURSDAY
OH, COME ON NOW!
CLANK
CLANK
AUTOBOTS, ROLL OUT!

ONLY ONE WAY TO FIND OUT

CAN'T SLEEP.
I'D READ BUT I DON'T WANT TO WAKE SELINE UP.
WHAT TO DO... WHAT TO DO...
I SUPPOSE I COULD PONDER THE MEANING OF LIFE AND OTHER MATTERS OF VAST IMPORTANCE...
I WONDER IF SHE'D WAKE UP IF I HAD SEX WITH HER...
I WONDER IF SHE'D BE PLEASED WITH MY INITIATIVE...

SLEEP"WALK"ING?

WHAT?
ARE YOU TRYING TO HAVE SEX WITH ME WHILE I'M SLEEPING?
I LOVE JUICE.

UP AND NOWHERE TO GO

SINCE YOU'RE UP...
GOOD NIGHT, RAYNE.
RELATIONSHIPS SUCK.
TRUE STORY.

ONCE UPON A RAYNE

I'M NOT HAPPY.
I GATHERED.
I WANTED TO HAVE SEX AND SELINE SAID NO!
YOU BELIEVE THAT?
MY GIRLFRIEND WOULDN'T PLEASURE ME WHEN I SO DESIRED.
IS THAT EVEN LEGAL?
ARE YOU KIDDING ME?
I MEAN I'VE HEARD TALES OF SUCH BUT I THOUGHT THEY WERE JUST URBAN LEGENDS...
LIKE ANOREXIA OR BULIMIA...

ABOUT TIME

IS THIS WHAT ALL RELATIONSHIPS ARE LIKE?
CONSTANT SEX AT THE BEGINNING, THEN IT SLOWLY LESSENS AS TIME PROGRESSES?
PRETTY MUCH.
I'M LUCKY IF IT HAPPENS A COUPLE TIMES A WEEK.
MY INSATIABLE SEX DRIVE CAN'T MAKE DUE ON TWICE A DAY.
I KNOW-
WAIT.
TWICE A DAY?
YOU'RE BITCHING ABOUT ONLY HAVING SEX TWICE A DAY?
WHAT I DO NOW, I DO FOR MONOGAMOUS MEN IN RELATIONSHIPS EVERYWHERE.
WHAT'S HAPPENING NOW?
I FELL DOWN SOME STAIRS.
NO, HE DIDN'T.
I BEAT THE $#+@ OUT OF HIM WITH A SMILE ON MY FACE.

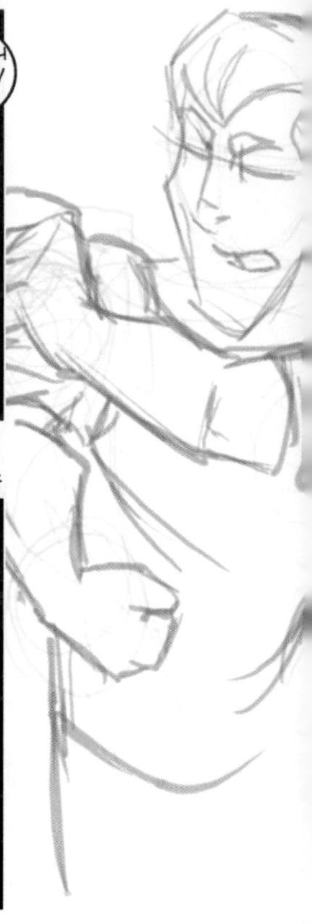

POUNCE!

THE WET RUN

I WISH I HAD CANDY PEE...

JOHN!
COME SMELL MY PEE!
IT SMELLS LIKE CANDY!
THANK YOU, NO.
SELINE!
COME SMELL MY CANDY PEE!
THAT'S REALLY GREAT, HONEY.
Relationship
Man-Whore

IT'S NOT FUNNY IF YOU HAVE TO EXPLAIN IT

DO YOU THINK WE TALK ENOUGH?
I THINK WE TALK PLENTY.
WE'RE TALKING RIGHT NOW.
BUT WE DON'T REALLY–
WHY ARE YOU GIGGLING?
I JUST THOUGHT OF SOMETHING FUNNY TO SAY TO NOEL ON OUR NEXT WALK.
"I SHOULD PUNCH YOU IN THE FEET".
WHY IN THE FEET?
COULDN'T TELL YOU.
SEE?
WE'RE TALKING AGAIN!
WE'RE AWESOME.

NO, NO – THANK YOU

QUIT STEWING AND TELL ME WHAT'S ON YOUR MIND.
SHE WON'T SHUT THE HELL UP!
SELINE?
YES!
AREN'T YOU PAYING ATTENTION?
I SHOULD PUNCH YOU IN THE FEET.
HOW CAN I HELP?
CAN YOU MAKE SELINE STOP TALKING ABOUT OUR RELATIONSHIP?
FOREVER?
PROBABLY NOT.
YOU KNOW THE GOLDEN GIRLS THEME SONG?
WELL, YOU ARE NEITHER A PAL NOR A CONFIDANTE.

CAN'T LIVE WITH 'EM

YOU DON'T WANT TO MEET MY PARENTS,
YOU DON'T WANT ME MEETING YOURS.
WE NEVER REALLY TALK ABOUT THINGS.
I DON'T KNOW WHAT YOU WANT FROM ALL OF THIS.
IT SEEMS LIKE ALL YOU EVER WANT TO DO IS HAVE SEX.
FEEL FREE TO STOP ME AT ANY TIME.
BELIEVE ME, I'M NOT SHY.
AS SOON AS YOU SAY SOMETHING I DISAGREE WITH, I'LL TOTALLY BE ALL UP IN YOUR FACE ABOUT IT.
I CAN'T DO THIS RIGHT NOW.
WHAT?
I'M ON YOUR SIDE HERE!

OH GEEEEEEZ...

THE TAO OF RAYNE
AFTER A DISAGREEMENT WITH YOUR SIGNIFICANT OTHER,
ORGY.
YAY OR NAY?
IT IS ALWAYS BEST TO TREAD LIGHTLY WHEN ATTEMPTING TO RE-OPEN THE LINES OF COMMUNICATION.

HALLMARK OR SKIDMARK?

HOW'S THE OLD BALL AND CHAIN?
I NEVER UNDERSTOOD WHAT THAT MEANT UNTIL VERY RECENTLY.
NICE TO SEE YOU'RE LEARNING SOMETHING.

I'VE TAKEN THAT NEWFOUND UNDERSTANDING AND CREATED A NEW ANALOGY FOR RELATIONSHIPS.

A RELATIONSHIP IS LIKE BEING TRAPPED IN A CAGE WITH A 1200 POUND GORILLA THAT FLINGS POOP AND WON'T LET YOU VAGINALLY PENETRATE-

YOU SHOULD WRITE GREETING CARDS.
THAT'S WHAT I'VE BEEN SAYING!

REACH OUT AND TOUCH SOMEONE

THIS RELATIONSHIP THING IS STRESSING ME OUT.
SELINE IS A LOT MORE SERIOUS THAN I AM, AND I'M STARTING TO FEEL A LITTLE BAD ABOUT IT.
I'M NOT EVEN ENJOYING THE SEX THAT MUCH ANYMORE,
I MOSTLY JUST DO IT SO WE CAN STOP TALKING.
ALWAYS WITH THE TALKING.
SOUNDS ROUGH.
LET ME BUY YOU A MASSAGE.
SARCASM IGNORED.
OFFER ACCEPTED.
I'LL GIVE YOU A MOMENT TO REALIZE HOW FORTUNATE YOU ARE.
THEN WE CAN BEGIN.

SEMI COLONIC

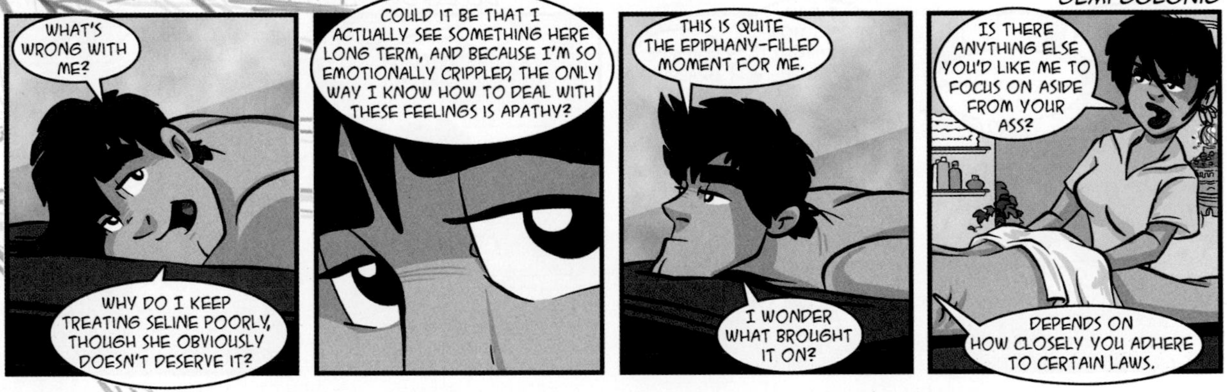

WHAT'S WRONG WITH ME?
WHY DO I KEEP TREATING SELINE POORLY, THOUGH SHE OBVIOUSLY DOESN'T DESERVE IT?
COULD IT BE THAT I ACTUALLY SEE SOMETHING HERE LONG TERM, AND BECAUSE I'M SO EMOTIONALLY CRIPPLED, THE ONLY WAY I KNOW HOW TO DEAL WITH THESE FEELINGS IS APATHY?
THIS IS QUITE THE EPIPHANY-FILLED MOMENT FOR ME.
I WONDER WHAT BROUGHT IT ON?
IS THERE ANYTHING ELSE YOU'D LIKE ME TO FOCUS ON ASIDE FROM YOUR ASS?
DEPENDS ON HOW CLOSELY YOU ADHERE TO CERTAIN LAWS.

JUST LIKE A MANLY MAN

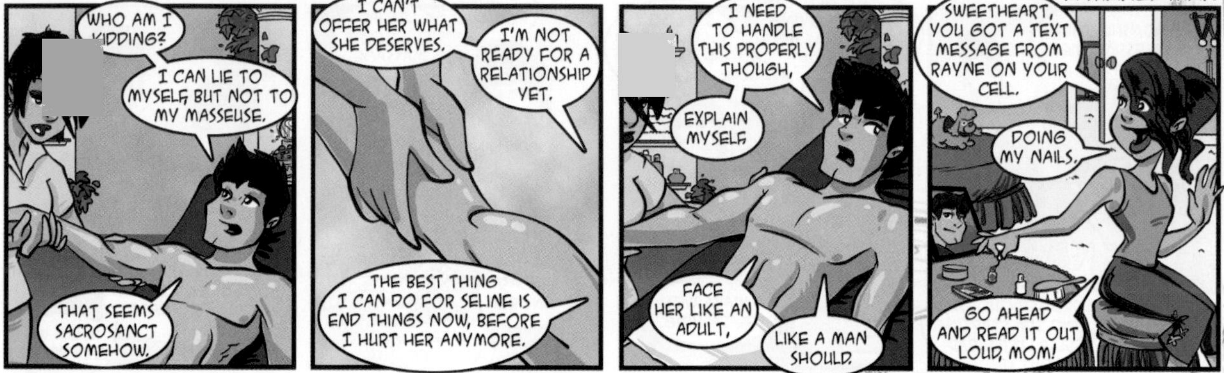
WHO AM I KIDDING?
I CAN LIE TO MYSELF, BUT NOT TO MY MASSEUSE.
THAT SEEMS SACROSANCT SOMEHOW.
I CAN'T OFFER HER WHAT SHE DESERVES.
I'M NOT READY FOR A RELATIONSHIP YET.
THE BEST THING I CAN DO FOR SELINE IS END THINGS NOW, BEFORE I HURT HER ANYMORE.
I NEED TO HANDLE THIS PROPERLY THOUGH,
EXPLAIN MYSELF
FACE HER LIKE AN ADULT,
LIKE A MAN SHOULD.
SWEETHEART, YOU GOT A TEXT MESSAGE FROM RAYNE ON YOUR CELL.
DOING MY NAILS.
GO AHEAD AND READ IT OUT LOUD, MOM!

DO DO DO DOWN DOOBIE DO DOWN, DOWN

YOU BROKE UP WITH SELINE?
IT WAS THE RIGHT THING TO DO.
-NG
I MAY REGRET HOW I WENT ABOUT IT, THOUGH.
YOU MIND GRABBING THAT?
RRRIIIIINNNNG
RIIIIINNNNG
CLIK
HEL-
COWARD!!!
I THINK IT'S FOR YOU.
ASK HER IF SHE GOT MY TEXT MESSAGE.

DO YOU LIKE APPLES?

HOW DID THE PHONE CONVERSATION GO?
I APOLOGIZED FOR MY METHOD OF BREAKING UP WHILE AT THE SAME TIME REMINDING HER OF ALL THE GOOD TIMES WE SHARED.
DID YOU FART?
NO.
YES.
BUT IT WAS TWENTY MINUTES AGO.
WHAT'S THE STATUTE OF LIMITATIONS ON CRIMES OF A GASEOUS NATURE?
OH MY GOD, RAYNE.
THAT'S HORRID.
APPARENTLY IT'S BEEN FERMENTING UNDER THE BLANKET EVER SINCE IT WAS RELEASED FROM MY ANUS.

100% TRANS FAT FREE

A TEXT MESSAGE?
REALLY.
WHY DIDN'T YOU JUST DUMP HER BY CARRIER PIGEON?
I DON'T WANT TO KNOW.
MAYBE WE SHOULD HAVE LAUNCHED THE PIGEONS FROM A WINDOW THAT WASN'T DIRECTLY FACING A POWER LINE?
USING THAT LOGIC, WE PROBABLY SHOULDN'T HAVE DIPPED THEM IN VEGETABLE OIL EITHER.
HINDSIGHT, H-UH?

NOT THE FACE!

YOU DID THE RIGHT THING, IN THE LONG RUN.
MAYBE, BUT I HANDLED IT POORLY AND TOOK THE EASY WAY OUT.
SO WHAT ARE YOU GOING TO DO?
WHAT I SHOULD HAVE DONE IN THE FIRST PLACE,
GO THERE IN PERSON AND EXPLAIN MYSELF.
I OWE IT TO HER.
NOT AFRAID SELINE WILL TAKE THE OPPORTUNITY TO STAB YOU?
LIKE MACGYVER AND JESUS BEFORE ME, I AM EVER PREPARED.
I WAS SLEEPING!
I KNOW MUNCHKIN, BUT UNCA NEEDS AN ADORABLE HUMAN SHIELD RIGHT NOW.
Don't kill my Unca
HOLD UP YOUR SIGN A LITTLE HIGHER.

FIELD TRIP

UNCA?
YES, MUNCHKIN?
THAT DIDN'T GO WELL, DID IT?
NO, IT DID NOT.
I DON'T THINK SELINE THINKS VERY HIGHLY OF ME RIGHT NOW.
UNCA?
YES, MUNCHKIN?
WHAT DOES
F#
MEAN?
IT MEANS UNCA IS GOING TO BE PAYING YOU HUSH MONEY FOR A LITTLE WHILE SO THAT YOUR PARENTS DON'T REVOKE HIS VISITING RIGHTS.

TO THINE OWN SELF

THAT'S IT FOR RELATIONSHIPS, THEN?
FOR NOW.
I'M JUST NOT IN THE SAME PLACE AS THE REST OF YOU, AND TO BE HONEST, I'M NOT SURE I EVER WILL BE.
I THINK I'M OKAY WITH THAT BECAUSE MY PLACE HAS THE POTENTIAL FOR AN ASIAN THEMED THREESOME,
WHILE YOURS IS EATING MAC AND CHEESE ON THE COUCH WATCHING THE HOME AND GARDEN NETWORK.
YOUR PLACE **SUCKS.**
I WAS GETTING THE GIST, THANKS.

HE'S BACK, BABY

YOU'RE CUTE, BUT I JUST GOT OUT OF A RELATIONSHIP AND DON'T THINK I'M READY FOR ANYTHING YET.

MAYBE TOGETHER, WE CO-
IT'S SILLY, FORGET IT.

MAYBE TOGETHER...
MAYBE TOGETHER, WE COULD HEAL BETTER THAN WE WOULD, EACH ON OUR OWN.
YOU MAKE ME NAUSEOUS.
WHY DON'T YOU WANT ME TO BE HAPPY AGAIN?

IG-NOBLE
YOU KNOW WHO I'M REALLY STARTING TO LIKE?
AL GORE.
HERE'S A GUY WHO THE PEOPLE ARE BEGGING TO RUN FOR PRESIDENT, AND WHAT DOES HE DO INSTEAD?
BLINK BLINK
HE DEVELOPS A WEAPON THAT IS SLOWLY DESTROYING THE ENVIRONMENT IN WHICH WE LIVE.
MORE SO, HE'S SPECIFICALLY TARGETING COASTAL REGIONS, IN WHAT I CAN ONLY ASSUME IS A REVENGE SCHEME ON FLORIDA FOR NOT UNDERSTANDING HOW TO VOTE.
THE BEST PART?
HE WINS A FREAKING NOBEL PEACE PRIZE FOR IT!
YOU NEED TO STOP READING THE NEWSPAPER WHILE WATCHING TV.
IT HAS TO BE ONE OR THE OTHER.
THAT'S LIKE THANKING THE CYLONS FOR THEIR CONTRIBUTIONS TO MANKIND!
WATCHOUTFORTHATTREE!
HAI!
HAI
OOOK.

HOT AS ICE

OUR HEADLINE STORY FOR THE DAY,
I HAVE TAKEN IT UPON MYSELF TO LIBERATE BRITNEY SPEARS' TWO CHILDREN FROM THE HORROR SHOW THAT IS THEIR MOTHER.
CURRENTLY, I HAVE THEM BOTH LOCKED IN A CAGE SURROUNDED BY DISEASE INFECTED TIGERS.
AND YET, THEY'RE STILL SAFER WITH ME.
NOW, FOR A LOOK AT THE WEATHER, HERE'S OUR SPECIAL CORRESPONDENT MICK ALFA, WHO'S ON THE SCENE IN CALIFORNIA.
FIRE!!!
MICK ALFA
SPECIAL CORRESPONDENT

END OF AN ERA

CAN I GET 1,000 COPIES OF MAXIM PLEASE?
THAT'S A LITTLE EXCESSIVE, NO?
WITH THE CURRENT AMOUNT OF IGNORANCE AND POLITICAL LEANINGS THAT'S PERMEATING MOST NEWS OUTLETS,
I FEEL THAT THE RARE ATTEMPT AT HONEST JOURNALISM SHOULD BE REWARDED.
e Five Unsexiest Women Alive
NICE JOB ON MAKING POLITICAL STATEMENTS AND BEING CRUEL AT THE SAME TIME.
I HAD TO MAKE NOTES, BUT OL' HORSE FACE WAS WORTH IT.

LICD
presents
Moments from the Bible
BY
CAR DESOUZA
ON TO THE PROMISED LAND!
HOLD UP THERE, SHEEP BOY.
IT SAYS HERE THAT YOUR SO CALLED PROMISED LAND IS GOING TO BE THE PREMIERE DESTINATION FOR WAR, VIOLENCE AND GENERAL UNEASE OVER THE NEXT FOUR THOUSAND YEARS.
THE CRUSADES SOUND LIKE THEY COULD BE A GOOD TIME.
FUH-LAMING!
GOD JUST SPOKE TO ME.
AS A FLAMING GRAIN OF SAND.
HE SAYS WE SHOULD HEAD TO HAWAII.
I'M A BARBIE GIRL IN A BARBIE WORLD
LIFE IN PLASTIC, IT'S FANTASTIC
YOU CAN BRUSH MY HAIR, UNDRESS ME EVERYWHERE
TASE 'EM, BRO!
AQUA IS REUNITING.
LEAVE THE CUFFS ON.

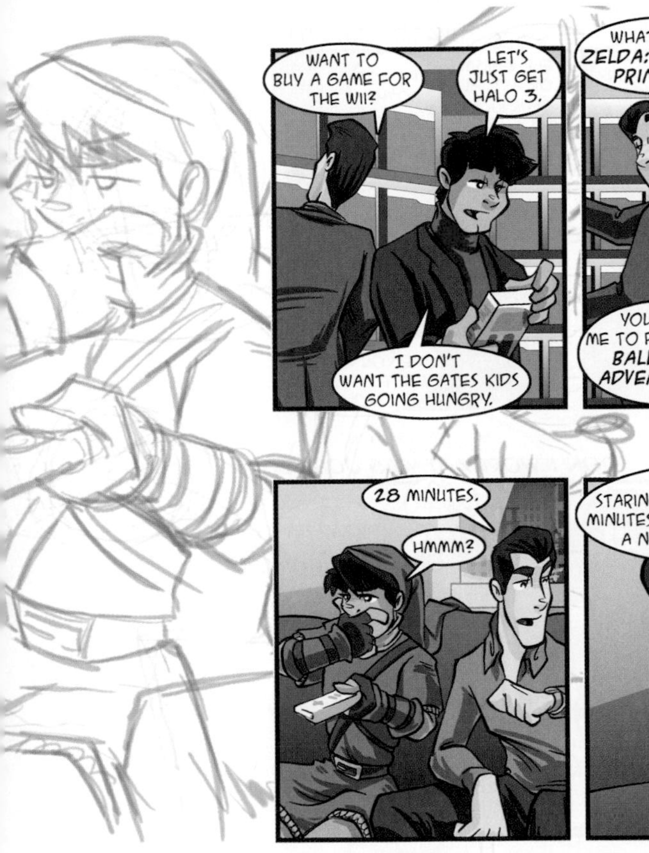

NOW IT MAKES SENSE

WANT TO BUY A GAME FOR THE WII?
LET'S JUST GET HALO 3.
I DON'T WANT THE GATES KIDS GOING HUNGRY.
WHAT ABOUT ZELDA: TWILIGHT PRINCESS?
FIGURES YOU'D LIKE A GAME WITH 'PRINCESS' IN THE TITLE.
YOU WANT ME TO PRE-ORDER BALLERINA ADVENTURES?
THE SPECIAL EDITION INCLUDES A LITTLE TUTU.
IT SAYS HERE YOU USE THE TWO CONTROLLERS
LIKE YOU'D SWING A SWORD OR HOLD A SHIELD.
YOU CAN EVEN BUY ACCESSORIES THAT LOOK AND FEEL LIKE THE WEAPONS.
I SEE.

I SAY "NEIGH-NEIGH"!

28 MINUTES.
HMMM?
YOU'VE BEEN STARING AT THE SCREEN FOR 28 MINUTES TRYING TO COME UP WITH A NAME FOR YOUR HORSE.
A WARRIOR'S STEED REQUIRES A NOBLE NAME.
28 MINUTES.
YEP.
I'M GOING TO GET A DRINK.
DO I SPELL HORSEY WITH AN 'EY' OR 'IE'?

WATCH OUT, TIM!
THANKS FOR THE SHIRT.
I WAS VIOLATED IN HYRULE.
MY PLEASURE.
BEEN THINKING ABOUT STARTING A WHOLE 'VIOLATED BY' CLOTHING LINE.
I THINK THE OPRAH ONE WOULD BE A HUGE SELLER.
PULL OUT YOUR SWORD.
THE EUPHEMISM OR ACTUAL SWORD?
I'VE GOT BOTH.
WHICHEVER ONE YOU WANT TO USE TO HIT THAT TROLL.
DON'T WORRY; IT WAS JOHN'S
WHAT DO YOU THINK?
ONLY ONE WAY TO FIND OUT.
SMASH
NO RUPEES.
WE SHOULD TRY A PLANT.
FOR SCIENTIFIC ACCURACY.

ARE YA' READY, KIDS?

REMEMBER THE TIME WE BEGAN PLAYING ZELDA HOPING TO HACK AND SLASH OUR WAY THROUGH A WORLD OF MAYHEM?
HERE FISHY, FISHY.
DO YOU RECALL WHEN INSTEAD WE WERE HANDED A FISHING ROD FROM A LITTLE BOY AND TOLD TO CATCH A COUPLE OF FISH SO THE SHOP LADY WOULD SELL US A SLINGSHOT?
FISHY, FISHY,
FISHY.
WHAT ABOUT THE TIME WHEN THE INSTRUCTIONS FOR FISHING WERE SO POORLY WRITTEN THAT WE JUST COULDN'T FIGURE IT OUT?
HERE FISHY, FISHY, FISHY, FISHY.
OR WHEN WE SAT IN FRONT OF THE TELEVISION FOR SIX HOURS STRAIGHT TRYING TO CATCH A VIRTUAL FISH?
FISHY!

R FOR RAYNE

WE'VE MET ZELDA IN NINE DIFFERENT GAMES, RIGHT?
AT LEAST.
THEN WHY DOES SHE ALWAYS PRETEND LIKE SHE HAS NO IDEA WHO WE ARE?
THEORIES?
LINK SLIPS HER A LITTLE GHB AT THE END OF EACH QUEST,
OR HE HITS HER IN THE HEAD WITH HIS BOOMERANG AND THE TRAUMA IS TOO MUCH FOR HER FRAGILE MEMORY TO HANDLE.
SO HE'S EITHER A WOMAN BEATER OR A DATE RAPIST?
PRETTY MUCH.
STRANGE THAT THE GAME IS RATED E FOR EVERYONE, H-UH?
NO MORE ZELDA FOR YOU.

BABY SOHMER
1988-2007

THINK OUTSIDE THE RUNS

YOU WILL REMEMBER ME, BEFORE THE END.
AAAAAAAAAAAAAH!
GLMPF!
SNRF!
GOBBLE!
TACO
I'M NOT GETTING YOU LUNCH ANYMORE.
BRING ON THE NEXT CHALLENGER!

WONG NUMBER

THAT WASN'T IN THE AGREEMENT.
YOU CAN'T SIMPLY ADD ON A TARIFF BECAUSE IT SUITS YOUR MOOD.
YOU WILL REMOVE THAT CHARGE IMMEDIATELY, OR JEBAS HELP YOU, I WILL PERSONALLY LEAD THE FORCE THAT CONQUERS AND ENSLAVES YOUR ENTIRE NATION.
HOW'D THE CALL GO WITH THE CHINESE CONSULATE GENERAL?
I MAY HAVE COMMITTED US TO AN INVASION.
CHINA'S PRETTY SPARSELY POPULATED, RIGHT?
HEY, WHILE WE'RE IN THE REGION, WE SHOULD GRAB INDIA TOO.

EXCELLENT PEOPLE SKILLS

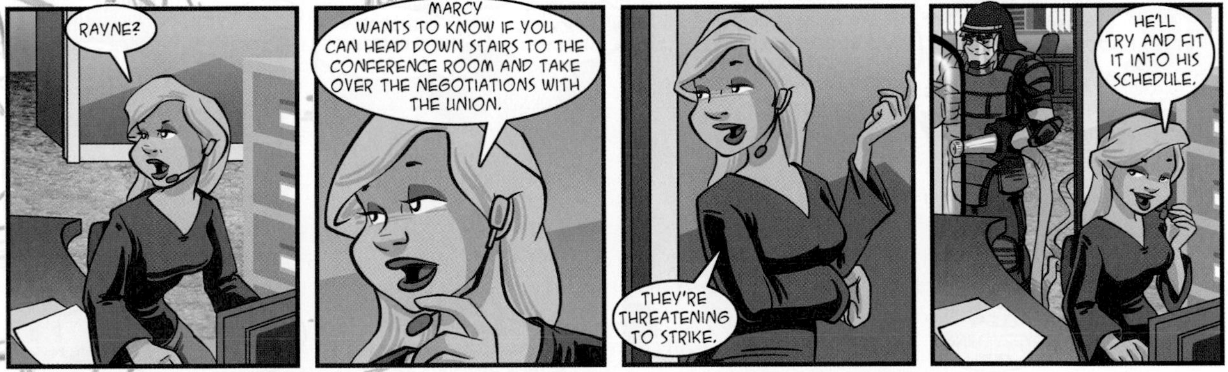

RAYNE?
MARCY WANTS TO KNOW IF YOU CAN HEAD DOWN STAIRS TO THE CONFERENCE ROOM AND TAKE OVER THE NEGOTIATIONS WITH THE UNION.
THEY'RE THREATENING TO STRIKE.
HE'LL TRY AND FIT IT INTO HIS SCHEDULE.

AN AIR OF COMMAND

MANAGEMENT PROMISED US-
WE SIMPLY CAN'T AFFORD IT-
FOR THOSE HERE THAT DON'T KNOW ME, I AM RAYNE SUMMERS, VP.
YOU CHILDREN COULDN'T FIND A SOLUTION ON YOUR OWN, SO MS MCKEAN SENT FOR A GROWN UP.
UNFORTUNATELY, NO ONE WAS AVAILABLE SO YOU'RE STUCK WITH ME.
MR SUMMERS-
BEFORE WE BEGIN, IN THE INTEREST OF FULL DISCLOSURE, I'D LIKE TO STATE THAT I HAD SIX TACOS FOR LUNCH.
AND THEY ARE NOT SITTING WELL.
NOW, WHO'D LIKE TO GO FIRST?

THAT'S HOW HE ROLLS...FOR INITIATIVE

THIS UNION REPRESENTS OVER 1,300 IDS EMPLOYEES, WORLDWIDE-
WHAT WE NEED TO DO HERE IS GET RID OF THIS TABLE, GET RID OF THESE CHAIRS.
CLEAR EVERYTHING OUT.
ONCE THAT'S DONE, WE'LL BRING IN TWO HORSES, TWO LANCES AND TWO SETS OF ARMOR.
ACTUALLY, FORGET THE ARMOR.
EACH SIDE WILL PICK THEIR CHAMPION,
PREFERABLY THEIR RESPECTIVE LEADERS.
THE VICTOR OF THE CHALLENGE WILL HAVE THEIR DEMANDS MET.
YOU...
YOU WANT US TO JOUST?
FOLLOWED BY MELEE COMBAT, YES.
FOR SOMEONE WITH A BIG BOOK OF NOTES, YOU'RE NOT REALLY 'WITH IT!'

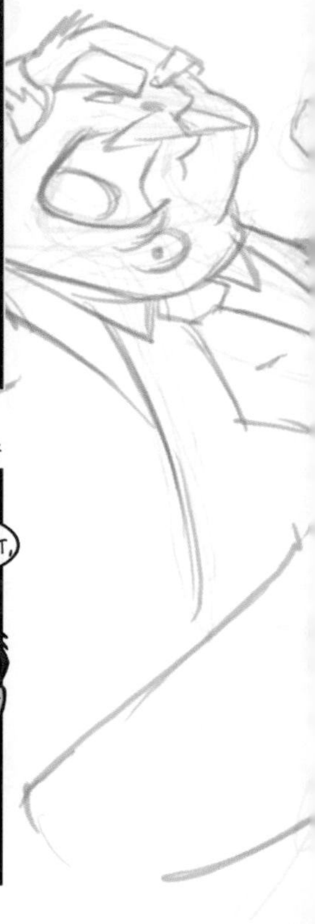

WILD RAGE RIDES AGAIN

I SPEAK ENGLISH VERY WELL...

ALRIGHT, BREAK IT DOWN FOR ME.
WHAT INCREASE ARE YOU LOOKING FOR?
FOUR PERCENT.
WHAT IS THE COMPANY PREPARED TO OFFER?
TWO PERCENT.
I SEE.
DID NO ONE THINK TO COMPROMISE AND MEET AT THREE PERCENT?
I DON'T UNDERSTAND.
I SAID FOUR PERCENT.

NOT HIS USUAL BANG

WHAT WE'RE ASKING FOR IS NOT UNREASONABLE, RAYNE.
THE COST OF LIVING INCREASES I CAN GET BEHIND, BUT THE REST OF THIS?
DOUBLE THE PERSONAL DAYS, RIDICULOUS CAPS ON OVERTIME, MINIMUM STAFFING REQUIREMENTS
THIS WOULD LEAD TO MASSIVE LAYOFFS IN SIX MONTHS.
THEN INSTEAD OF SHORTCHANGING YOUR WORKERS, YOU SHOULD BE INCREASING SALES.
I CAN'T BELIEVE YOU'RE MAKING ME SIDE WITH BIG BUSINESS
WE DON'T WANT TO STRI-
NANCY?
CAN YOU GET ME DICK CHENEY, A RIFLE AND A MILDLY SARCASTIC APOLOGY SPEECH PLEASE?
MAKE SURE THE SPEECH INCLUDES ADEQUATE PAUSES FOR UNDER MY BREATH CHUCKLING.

YOUR MILEAGE MAY VARY

IT'S FUN FOR THE WHOLE FAMILY.

WE'RE PREPARED FOR A STRIKE-
YOU'VE STATED THAT.
I'M GOING TO BE BRUTALLY HONEST WITH YOU RIGHT NOW.
WE DO NOT WANT A STRIKE,
IT WOULD COST US MONEY.
HOWEVER, IT'S MONEY WE COULD AFFORD.
FRANKLY PUT, THIS COMPANY CAN HOLD OUT A LOT LONGER THAN YOUR GUYS CAN.
YOU SAY THAT NOW, WE'LL SEE HOW-
LET'S PLAY A LITTLE GAME I ENJOY WHILE DRIVING CALLED 'YIELD TO ME, [redacted]'

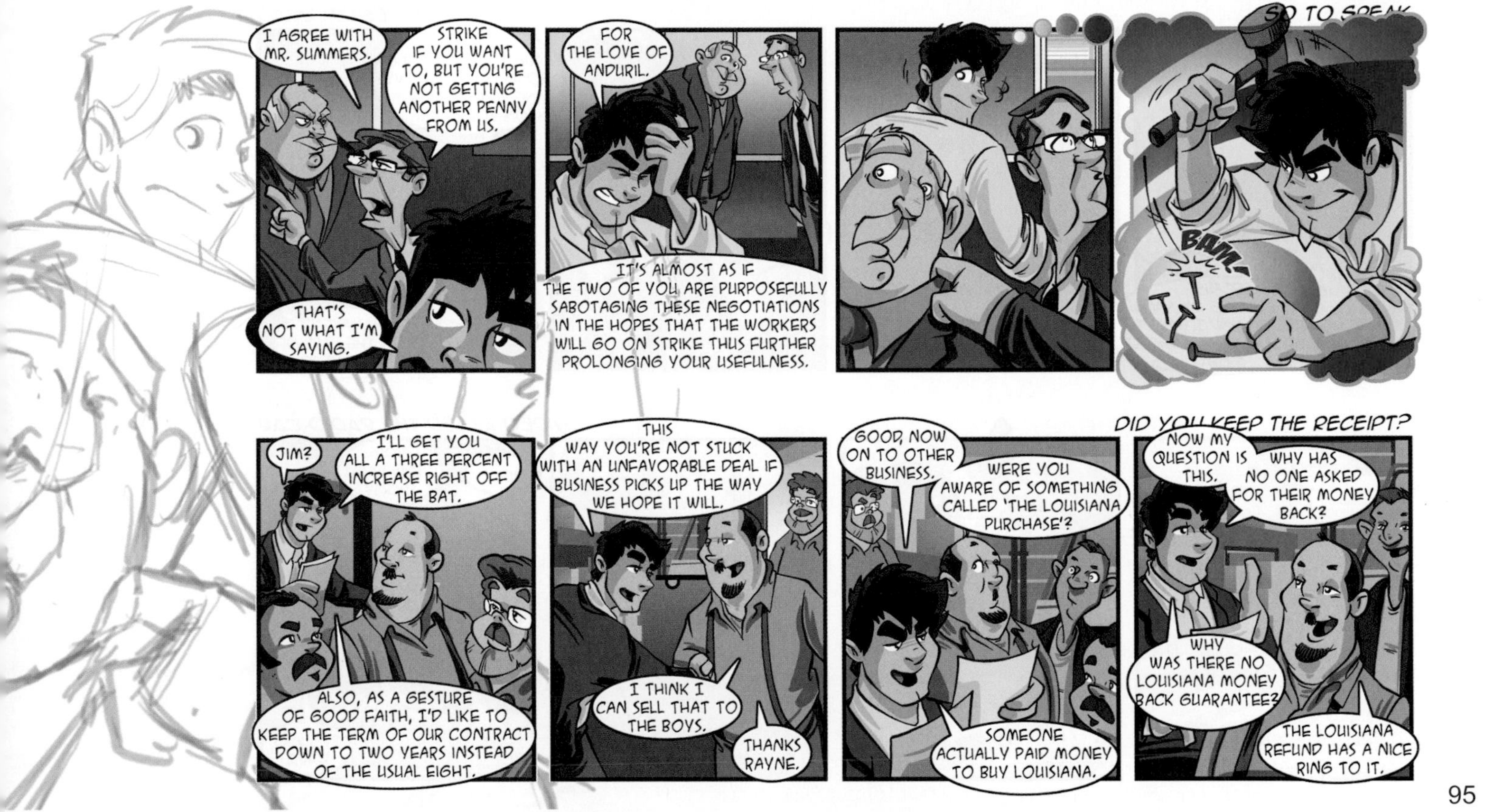

SO TO SPEAK
I AGREE WITH MR. SUMMERS.
STRIKE IF YOU WANT TO, BUT YOU'RE NOT GETTING ANOTHER PENNY FROM US.
THAT'S NOT WHAT I'M SAYING.
FOR THE LOVE OF ANDURIL.
IT'S ALMOST AS IF THE TWO OF YOU ARE PURPOSEFULLY SABOTAGING THESE NEGOTIATIONS IN THE HOPES THAT THE WORKERS WILL GO ON STRIKE THUS FURTHER PROLONGING YOUR USEFULNESS.
BAM!
DID YOU KEEP THE RECEIPT?
JIM?
I'LL GET YOU ALL A THREE PERCENT INCREASE RIGHT OFF THE BAT.
ALSO, AS A GESTURE OF GOOD FAITH, I'D LIKE TO KEEP THE TERM OF OUR CONTRACT DOWN TO TWO YEARS INSTEAD OF THE USUAL EIGHT.
THIS WAY YOU'RE NOT STUCK WITH AN UNFAVORABLE DEAL IF BUSINESS PICKS UP THE WAY WE HOPE IT WILL.
I THINK I CAN SELL THAT TO THE BOYS.
THANKS RAYNE.
GOOD, NOW ON TO OTHER BUSINESS.
WERE YOU AWARE OF SOMETHING CALLED 'THE LOUISIANA PURCHASE'?
SOMEONE ACTUALLY PAID MONEY TO BUY LOUISIANA.
NOW MY QUESTION IS THIS.
WHY HAS NO ONE ASKED FOR THEIR MONEY BACK?
WHY WAS THERE NO LOUISIANA MONEY BACK GUARANTEE?
THE LOUISIANA REFUND HAS A NICE RING TO IT.

ALTER EGOMANIAC

WHY AM I DRIVING YOU TO WORK AGAIN?
BECAUSE I'M GETTING MY SNOW TIRES ON AND I HAVE TO GET TO PARENT TEACHER NIGHT.
BECAUSE I CAUGHT YOU CUTTING HOLES IN MY PILLOWS AND WEARING THEM ON YOUR HEAD.
YOU HAVEN'T SEEN THE LAST OF PILLOWHEAD.

VIDEO KILLED THE RADIO CAR

VRRRRMMMM
BAM!
SMASH!!
HOLY-
YOU KNOW WHAT SUCKS?
RADIO SUCKS.
IT SUCKS HARD.

WELCOME TO SCENIC MORDOR

WHAT ARE YOU DOING?
GOING TO MAKE SURE THOSE PEOPLE ARE OKAY.
AND BREATHING.
YOU COMING?
ARE YOU CRAZY?
YOU'RE GOING TO TRY AND CROSS THE HIGHWAY?
YOU'LL GET KILLED!
I'M TOTALLY VOTING YOU OUT OF THE FELLOWSHIP LATER.
SURVIVOR
MIDDLE-EARTH
I'M SORRY, BUT PIPPIN'S JUST NOT CARRYING HIS WEIGHT.
I MEAN SERIOUSLY, I KILLED 70 URUK-HAI YESTERDAY WHILE HE HID IN THE BUSHES.
Pippin!
WHAT IS THAT ABOUT?

URETHRA FRANKLIN

WAAAAAAAAAAAAAAAAAAAAAAAAAAAAAAAAAAAA
I THINK I JUST PEED A LITTLE.
THE GOOD NEWS IS THAT THE INSTANT MY PEE LEFT THE URETHRA, IT FROZE ON ATMOSPHERIC CONTACT.
DID YOU JUST USE URETHRA IN A SENTENCE?
SOUNDS MORE LIKE SOMETHING FOUND IN A WOMAN THAN A MAN, NO?

IT'S NOT EASY

VOOOM
I'M RIDING A CROCODILE.
THIS IS WHY I STAYED IN THE CAR!

ONCE GOOD. TWICE BETTER.

HEY-
YOU GUYS OKAY?
YOU NEED TO SHUT YOUR ENGINE OFF PLEASE.
DOOR...
STUCK...
SMASH
SMASH

THAT'S GOOD ENOUGH FOR ME

CAR'S SHUT OFF..
NOW WHAT?
THINK. THINK.
THERE ARE TWO THINGS I LEARNED WATCHING ER, GRAY'S ANATOMY AND SESAME STREET.
THE FIRST IS NEVER, EVER, MOVE A TRAUMA VICTIM.
THE SECOND IS C IS FOR COOKIE.
BUT I'M NOT SURE HOW THAT APPLIES TO THE CURRENT SITUATION.
WHY IS THE CAR ROLLING BACK OUT INTO THE HIGHWAY?

MAYBE THE NEXT CAN

RAYNE!
THE CAR!
I'M ON IT.
RAYNE!
THE CAR!
FALSE ADVERTISING SHOULD BE A CRIME PUNISHABLE BY THROAT PUNCHES.

THE THERAPIST STRIKES BACK

RAYNE!
THERE'S A CAR COMING TOWARDS YOU!
LET'S SEE JESUS DO THIS.
IF I'D HAD THE INFORMATION I HAVE NOW JUST A FEW SECONDS EARLIER, THE PRESENT WOULD LOOK A LOT DIFFERENT.
YOU'RE PROBABLY GOING TO NEED A THERAPIST AFTER WITNESSING THE GRUESOME DEATH OF A CHILDHOOD FRIEND.
IT'S COOL.
I KNOW A GUY.

WHISKEY TANGO FOXTROT

ARE YOU OKAY, MA'AM?

WE BOTH ARE.
BUT WHAT ABOUT THE MAN WHO HELPED US?
I'M AFRAID HE'S NOT WITH US ANYMORE.

HE'S OVER THERE.
HE STOLE ALL OF OUR ROAD FLARES AND IS NOW TRYING TO LAND 747S.

TURN OFF THE AUTOPILOT AND LOOK DOWN, YOU SONS OF BITCHES!

UNUSUAL WEATHER WE'RE HAVING, AIN'T IT?

I WANTED TO THANK YOU FOR WHAT YOU DID-
YOU WEREN'T DRUNK DRIVING, WERE YOU?
NO!
WE SLIPPED ON BLACK ICE-
DO YOU OWN ANY APPLE PRODUCTS?
ARE YOU A BORN AGAIN VIRGIN?
NO.
WELL...
I HAVE AN IPOD.
IF I RISKED MY LIFE FOR A DRUNK CRAZY CHRISTIAN HIPPY, I'D BE LESS THAN PLEASED.
HEY!
WHERE SHOULD HE GO TO PICK UP HIS KEY TO THE CITY?
LOOK WHO FINALLY CAME OUT OF THE CAR!
WHO'S MY BWAVE WITTLE BOY?

SCENT OF PINING

I ALMOST DIED TODAY.
I HEARD.
I ALSO HEARD THERE WAS A CAR COMING RIGHT AT YOU, BUT NOT HOW YOU MANAGED TO AVOID IT.
I STOPPED IT WITH THE FORCE.
IT WAS CRUSHED AGAINST MY ERECTION.
THERE WAS NO CAR.
ENOUGH.
IT CAME WITHIN AN INCH OF ME BEFORE THE DRIVER WAS ABLE TO VEER OFF.
NARROWLY.
YOU'VE HAD NEAR MISSES BEFORE,
WHY ARE YOU SO SHAKEN UP AND PRETENDING NOT TO BE?
IT WAS A STUPID THING I DID, BUT IT WAS THE RIGHT THING.
AND?
JOHN WASN'T THERE.
HE'S NEVER THERE.

GREETINGS, PROFESSOR FALKEN

WE HAD OUR YEARLY SEXUAL HARASSMENT SEMINAR THIS MORNING.
HOW'D THAT GO?
YOU HAVE A QUESTION, MR SUMMERS?
WE HAVE A LITTLE GAME WE LIKE TO PLAY AROUND THE OFFICE, AND I WANTED TO MAKE SURE THAT WAS ALLOWED.
WE'RE NOT HERE TO ELIMINATE WORK PLACE CAMARADERIE–
IT'S CALLED 'UNDO MY ZIPPER!'
SHE GOING TO SETTLE OUT OF COURT?
I'D ASSUME SO.
HEY,
WANT TO PLAY A GAME?

WE HOLD THESE BOOBS

LICD presents MOMENTS IN HISTORY
WHAT DO YOU THINK OF THIS AMENDMENT?
"A WELL REGULATED MILITIA BEING NECESSARY TO THE SECURITY OF A FREE STATE, THE RIGHT OF THE PEOPLE TO KEEP AND BEAR ARMS SHALL NOT BE INFRINGED!"
IT'S ALRIGHT, BUT WHAT ABOUT CHANGING 'ARMS' FOR 'BREASTS!'
WHAT?
OF COURSE NOT!
200 YEARS FROM NOW, YOU'RE GOING TO WISH WE HAD GONE WITH BREASTS.
TONIGHT'S STORY:
MISUNDERSTOOD TEEN ON RAMPAGE.
VICTIMS WERE SLAPPED WITH BREASTS BUT ARE IN STABLE CONDITION.
AND ALIVE.

HANNUKAH? HANNU-CAN'T.

I WENT TO SYNAGOGUE ON SATURDAY.
YOU'RE NOT JEWISH.
NO, BUT I ENJOY THEIR DELICIOUS BREAD AND CHOCOLATE COINS.
MAKE ANY FRIENDS?
I BOW BEFORE NO ONE!
HEY, SO WHERE DO I GO TO GET THAT DELICIOUS BREAD AND THOSE CHOCOLATE COINS?

AND STILL NO JOHN

I KNOW WE'VE BEEN A LITTLE CONTROVERSIAL THIS WEEK,
SO TO SOOTHE THINGS, I THOUGHT IT BEST IF FOR TODAY, YOU WATCHED ME HUG MY CAT.
IF WE GOT RID OF OUR DEPENDENCE ON OIL BY DEVELOPING ALTERNATIVE FUEL SOURCES, PUTTING IN THE SAME AMOUNT OF MONEY WE PUT INTO DESTROYING ALASKA, WE WOULD REMOVE THE DEPENDENCY WE HAVE ON THE MIDDLE EAST AND SOUTH AMERICA, THUS CHANGING THE INTERNATIONAL LANDSCAPE FOR THE BETTER.
I RUINED IT, DIDN'T I?

I RUINED IT.

OF COURSE!

WE FINALLY GOT YOU.
DON'T MOVE!
WHAT'S THIS?
COBRA! RETREAT!
I KNEW IT.

MISCHIEF, MAYHEM, SOAP.

HYPOTHETICALLY, IF YOU WERE IN PRISON-
I LIKE WHERE THIS IS GOING.
IF YOU WERE IN PRISON, AND YOU WERE ACCOSTED BY A LARGE FELLOW-
WHY CAN'T I JUST DO MY TIME?
A LARGE FELLOW WHO PLANS ON VIOLATING YOU BY DROPPING THE SOAP AND ENCOURAGING YOU TO PICK UP THAT VERY SAME SOAP-
THERE A QUESTION?
DURING SAID VIOLATION, WOULD YOU LOOK BACK AT THE GUY TO MAKE EYE CONTACT OR KEEP YOUR FACE FORWARD?
WHAT'S THE ETIQUETTE THERE?
YOU'RE GOING TO MAKE SOMEONE VERY HAPPY ONE DAY.

HOW MUCH IS 'WOW'?

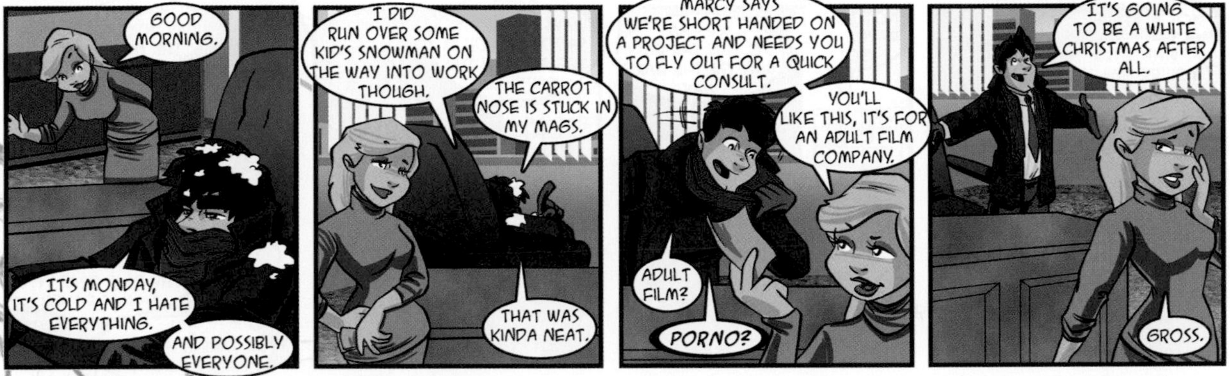

GOOD MORNING.
IT'S MONDAY, IT'S COLD AND I HATE EVERYTHING.
AND POSSIBLY EVERYONE.
I DID RUN OVER SOME KID'S SNOWMAN ON THE WAY INTO WORK THOUGH.
THE CARROT NOSE IS STUCK IN MY MAGS.
THAT WAS KINDA NEAT.
MARCY SAYS WE'RE SHORT HANDED ON A PROJECT AND NEEDS YOU TO FLY OUT FOR A QUICK CONSULT.
YOU'LL LIKE THIS, IT'S FOR AN ADULT FILM COMPANY.
ADULT FILM?
PORNO?
IT'S GOING TO BE A WHITE CHRISTMAS AFTER ALL.
GROSS.

DON'T. STOP.

NOEL, A 27 PAGE FAX JUST CAME IN FOR YOU.
WHAT'S ON THE COVER PAGE?
GOING TO LA. STOP.
PORNO SHOOT. STOP.
MEET ME AT AIRPORT. STOP.
BOOBIES. STOP.
BOOBIES. STOP.
BOOBIES. STOP.
BOOBIES...
IT GOES ON LIKE THIS.
HOW DOES HE HAVE MY FAX NUMBER?
BECAUSE I INSTALLED KEY LOGGING SOFTWARE ON YOUR COMPUTER THREE MONTHS AGO.
LET'S GO SEE BOOBIES. STOP.

DON'T TRANK ME, BRO!

NO.
WHATEVER YOU'RE SMILING AT, THE ANSWER IS NO.
NOT TODAY, RAYNE, I'VE GOT-
WE CAN DO THIS THE EASY WAY OR THE HARD WAY.
BOTH WAYS INVOLVE ME SHOOTING YOU IN THE ASS WITH THIS DART GUN.
WHICH WAY INVOLVES THE NET?
NOT SURE.
I DIDN'T REALLY INCORPORATE THE BEAR TRAP INTO THINGS EITHER.
HI, IT'S MICK.
I'LL BE TAKING A COUPLE PERSONAL DAYS.

LIGHTS! CAMERA! CHLAMYDIA!

PLEASE LET ME GO WITH RAYNE TO SEE THE PORNO SHOOT IN LA.
IN RETURN, I WILL LOSE THE AMOUNT OF WEIGHT THAT DIRECTLY CORRESPONDS TO HOW ANGRY YOU ARE.
YES, IT'S FOR THE ADULT FILM INDUSTRY,
BUT FROM WHAT HE'S PAYING ME, I'LL BE ABLE TO BUY YOU SOMETHING NICE FOR THE HOLIDAYS.
GOING TO SEE A PORNO, GOING TO SEE A PORNO.
DIDN'T CARE THE FIRST TEN TIMES YOU TOLD ME.
I HOPE YOU COME BACK WITH HEPATITIS.
DON'T WORRY, I'LL BRING YOU BACK SOMETHING TOO.

TO SEE WHAT HE COULD SEE
"BUMP"
ROCKIES
AND THAT'S WHY WE'RE TAKING THE PLANE INSTEAD OF TOBOGGANING ALL THE WAY TO CALIFORNIA.
YOU'RE STUPID AND I HATE YOU.
ANOTHER BAILEY'S, SIR?
PLEASE.
CASHEW? GESUNDHEIT!
IDS BUILDS THE CHIPS THAT ARE IN THE NEW CROP OF HD VIDEO CAMERAS,
AND ONE OF OUR CLIENTS SELLS EXCLUSIVELY TO THE PORN MARKET.
ONE OF HIS CLIENTS IS HAVING SOME ISSUES, AND THAT'S WHO WE'RE SEEING.
WHAT'S THE NAME OF THAT COMPANY?
FAT LADY GOAT PRODUCTIONS.
THEY SPECIALIZE IN GENRE PORN, I THINK.
SOMETHING TO DO WITH FAT LADY GOATS—
VIVID. WE'RE GOING TO VIVID.
JUST PUT THE NUT AWAY!
NICE.
I FORGOT ABOUT HIS ALLERGY.
I THINK I HAVE A WALNUT SOMEWHERE TOO.

BRAND NEW FACES

AFTER MUCH STUDY, I'VE COME UP WITH A SLOGAN THAT WILL ACCURATELY DEPICT YOUR COMPANY AT THE SAME TIME AS REACHING OUT TO A WHOLE NEW AUDIENCE.
VIVID ENTERTAINMENT GROUP
VIVID ENTERTAINMENT: WE LIKEM DEM TITTIES
I THOUGHT YOU WERE HERE TO HELP US WITH OUR HD RECORDING?
AND I THOUGHT I MADE IT VERY CLEAR THAT I AM AT A PORNO COMPANY AND THUS REFUSE TO TALK TO MEN.
COULD BE WHAT JENNA JAMESON LOOKS LIKE WITHOUT THE AIRBRUSHING?
THANKS FOR RUINING MANY HOURS OF FUTURE MASTURBATION.

JINGLED BALLS

THIS IS BRIANA BANKS.
I'VE ASKED HER TO SHOW YOU AROUND AND BRING YOU TO THE SET.
HI GUYS.
WHAM
DID THE WEIGHT OF HIS ERECTION ACTUALLY JUST CAUSE HIM TO FALL OVER?
SON OF A BITCH THAT HURT.
I WOULD'VE PREFERRED LANDING ON MY FACE.

TWICE ASS GOOD

THIS FLOOR HOUSES OUR SALES AND MARKETING TEAM-
DO YOU ENJOY DP AS MUCH AS YOU PORTRAY ON SCREEN?
SEEMS TO ME IT WOULD KINDA HURT.
DOUBLE PENETRATION.
I KNOW WHAT DP IS.
ding
ONE PENIS-
I KNOW!
I THINK SHE KNOWS.
SHE'S PRETTY SHY FOR SOMEONE WHO HAS SEX FOR A LIVING.
WHAT'S DP?

FIRE IN THE HOLE

THIS IS ONE OF OUR LIVE SETS, AND OUR TOP DIRECTOR.
WELCOME.
PLEASE BE CAREFUL WHILE YOU'RE HERE,
PORN SETS CAN BE A RATHER DANGEROUS SETTING.
INCOMING CUM SHOT!
GET DOWN!
SORRY,
THAT'S A LITTLE JOKE WE LIKE TO PLAY ON NEW PEOPLE.
DID YOU CONSIDER TAKING THE HIT FOR US, EVEN FOR A SPLIT SECOND?
DON'T MAKE THIS AWKWARD.

ONLY GAME IN TOWN

I THINK MY TEAM BUILDING INITIATIVES WOULD REALLY THRIVE IN THIS TYPE OF ENVIRONMENT.
OH?
THINKING OF IMPORTING 'UNZIP MY FLY' TO THE GOOD FOLKS AT VIVID?
NAH, THAT'S IN THE PAST.
I CAME UP WITH A NEW GAME.
IT'S CALLED 'PUT IT IN MY MOUTH'.
WHEN WE GET HOME, I'M BUYING YOU MONOPOLY.
WHAT YOU DO WITH THE SHOE AND THE THIMBLE WHILE THE OLD GUY IS WATCHING IS NONE OF MY BUSINESS.
WHY IS NOBODY WATCHING THE SEX??

THE DAVINCI LOAD

RAYNE SEEMS TO BE ENJOYING THE SPREAD AND THE COMPANY HERE.
YEAH, I THINK THIS IS BECOMING SOMETHING OF A RELIGIOUS EXPERIENCE FOR HIM.
RELIGIOUS?
WHAT MAKES YOU SAY THAT?
I DON'T KNOW EXACTLY, BUT I CAN'T SHAKE THE FEELING.
HENCEFORTH, I WILL REFER TO YOU BY YOUR BREAST SIZES ONLY.
DD, CAN I GET A LITTLE MORE WINE?

SMELLS LIKE FISH

WHAT'S THE PROBLEM?
YOUR FEMALE PERFORMERS ARE LAZY.
LOOK AT THIS GIRL.
SHE'S JUST LYING THERE LIKE A DEAD FISH.
I'VE SEEN MORE AROUSING BEHAVIOR OUT OF MICK ATTACKING A BAG OF CHIPS.
IT'S TRUE.
I MEANT, WHAT'S THE PROBLEM WITH THE HD CAMERAS?
I FIXED THAT SIX HOURS AGO.
MOVE YOUR ! HIPS A LITTLE!
I HAVE AN IDEA HOW TO PROMOTE MOVEMENT.
YOU HAVE A CATTLE PROD ON SET?

NOT BAD FOR A START

WE INTERRUPT THIS STORYLINE TO BRING YOU:
RAYNE'S NEW YEAR'S RESOLUTION 2008
I RESOLVE TO IMPROVE MYSELF IN EVERY CONCEIVABLE WAY.

FROM RUSSIA WITH LUST

OVER HERE, WE'RE SHOOTING A FILM ABOUT ORAL SEX FEATURING INTERNATIONAL ACTRESSES.
IN SOVIET RUSSIA, VAGINA EATS YOU.
I VOTED FOR VLADMIR PUTIN AS PERSON OF THE YEAR.
NICE TO SEE MULTICULTURALISM COME TO THE PORN INDUSTRY.
IF SHE HAD SAID 'VAGOO', SHE WOULD'VE OWED BOTH YAKOV SMIRNOFF AND ME ROYALTIES.

PARK AVENUE

YOU'RE SURPRISING ME.
YOU AVERAGE PEOPLE ARE ALWAYS IMPRESSED SO EASILY.
US SPECIALS CALL YOU 'NORMIES', YOU KNOW.
FINISHED?
NOT SURE.
KEEP GOING AND I'LL INTERRUPT AS NEEDED.
I'M SURPRISED YOU HAVEN'T BEEN TRYING HARDER TO SLEEP WITH ANYONE HERE.
I WAS PLANNING ON IT, BUT SOMETHING ABOUT THIS PLACE IS TELLING ME THAT'S NOT THE BEST IDEA.
ONSITE HIV TESTING
LAB HOURS
M-F: 08:30-16:30
WEIRD.
I KNOW, RIGHT?

GAZONGA GODDESS

CAN I ASK YOU A PROFESSIONAL QUESTION?
SURE.
IT'S CLEAR THAT YOUR BREASTS WERE NOT PART OF GOD'S MASTER PLAN.
NOR ARE THEY SENTIENT LIFE FORMS WHO'VE EXPERIENCED NATURAL EVOLUTION OVER THE COURSE OF MILLENNIA.
I'M ALSO PRETTY SURE THAT YOU WEREN'T IN AN ACCIDENT REQUIRING THE GOVERNMENT TO REBUILD YOU,
WHILE UPPING YOUR CUP SIZE DURING THE BIONIC AUGMENTATIONS.
WHAT'S THE QUESTION?
CAN I SEE THEM?

PIZZAS, HOT TUBS AND BIMBOS

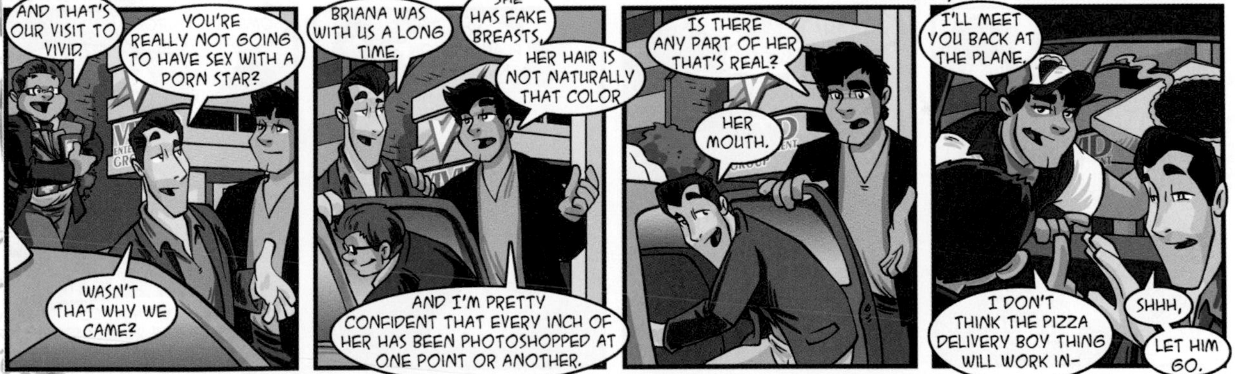

AND THAT'S OUR VISIT TO VIVID.
YOU'RE REALLY NOT GOING TO HAVE SEX WITH A PORN STAR?
WASN'T THAT WHY WE CAME?
BRIANA WAS WITH US A LONG TIME.
SHE HAS FAKE BREASTS,
HER HAIR IS NOT NATURALLY THAT COLOR
AND I'M PRETTY CONFIDENT THAT EVERY INCH OF HER HAS BEEN PHOTOSHOPPED AT ONE POINT OR ANOTHER.
IS THERE ANY PART OF HER THAT'S REAL?
HER MOUTH.
I'LL MEET YOU BACK AT THE PLANE.
I DON'T THINK THE PIZZA DELIVERY BOY THING WILL WORK IN-
SHHH,
LET HIM GO.

POST EPIPHANY

YOU HAVEN'T MENTIONED ANYTHING ABOUT THE UPCOMING AMERICAN PRESIDENTIAL ELECTIONS.
MEH.
I'D RATHER FOCUS MY ENERGY ON ELECTIONS THAT ACTUALLY MATTER.
RAYNE FOR JESUS '08

WITH GREAT POWER

HEY, DID YOU-
AAAAH!
SPIDER!
YEP.
YOU PLANNING ON KILLING IT?
NOT UNTIL IT BITES ME AT LEAST ONCE.
THERE'S SOMETHING WRONG WITH YOU.
SAY THAT WHEN I'M WEBBING AROUND THE CITY.
IF YOU WANT TO SEE SOMETHING REALLY SPECIAL, YOU SHOULD WATCH HIM LICK THE MICROWAVE.

ONLY DURING THUNDERSTORMS

KATE AND I HAVE BEEN DISCUSSING THE FUTURE,
ESPECIALLY THE IDEA OF KIDS ONE DAY.
AS IN HAVING THEM OR SELLING THEM?
SHE WANTS SIX KIDS.
WHEN I TOLD HER THAT I WANTED TWO, SHE SAID THAT WASN'T ENOUGH.
ENOUGH FOR WHAT?
DOES SHE THINK YOU'RE GOING TO BE THE VON TRAPP FAMILY?
HEH.
WE ABOUT TO DO WHAT I THINK WE'RE GOING TO DO?
LOOKS THAT WAY.
THE HILLS ARE ALIVE, WITH THE SOUND OF MUSIC...

A MAN NEEDS A LITTLE MADNESS

I DIDN'T REALIZE YOU WERE TAKING ME TO SUCH A NICE GREEK RESTAURANT TONIGHT.
THIS IS A TREAT.
CAN I GET YOU ANYTHING FOR DESSERT?
WHAT WOULD YOU RECOMMEND, KEREN?
THE HONEY BALLS ARE DELICIOUS.
Keren
THE HONEY BALLS, YOU SAY?
I BELIEVE MY FRIEND HERE THOROUGHLY ADORES HONEY BALLS.
SHE LIKES TO SAVOR THEM IN HER MOUTH, I BELIEVE.
A $150 DINNER JUST SO YOU COULD SAY HONEY BALLS?
REALLY?
WOULD ANYONE CARE TO JOIN US IN ENJOYING MY SUCCULENT HONEY BALLS?

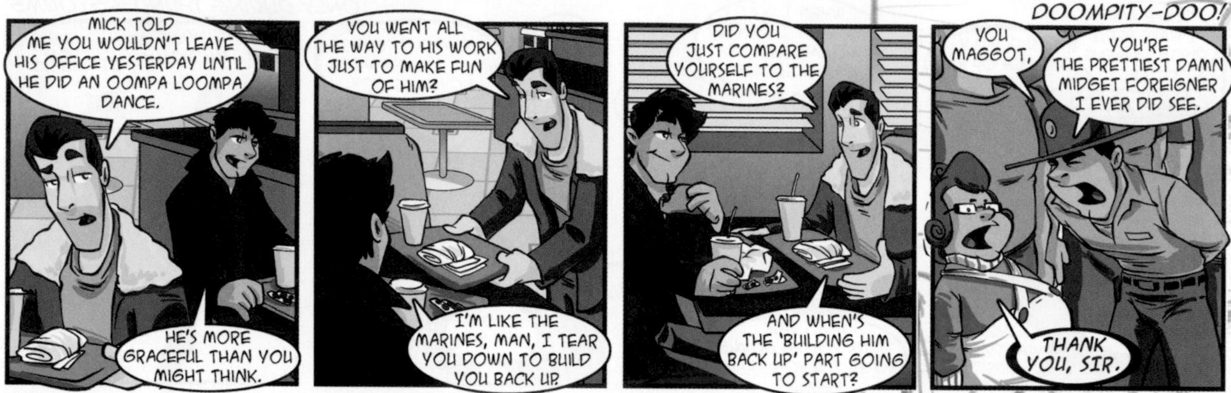
DOOMPITY-DOO!
MICK TOLD ME YOU WOULDN'T LEAVE HIS OFFICE YESTERDAY UNTIL HE DID AN OOMPA LOOMPA DANCE.
HE'S MORE GRACEFUL THAN YOU MIGHT THINK.
YOU WENT ALL THE WAY TO HIS WORK JUST TO MAKE FUN OF HIM?
I'M LIKE THE MARINES, MAN, I TEAR YOU DOWN TO BUILD YOU BACK UP.
DID YOU JUST COMPARE YOURSELF TO THE MARINES?
AND WHEN'S THE 'BUILDING HIM BACK UP' PART GOING TO START?
YOU MAGGOT,
YOU'RE THE PRETTIEST DAMN MIDGET FOREIGNER I EVER DID SEE.
THANK YOU, SIR.

DON'T BE STUPID, BE A SMARTIE
I MET THIS GIRL ONLINE, AND WE WERE EXCHANGING E-MAILS FOR THE LAST COUPLE OF WEEKS.
BUT I HAVEN'T HEARD ANYTHING BACK IN DAYS AFTER MY LAST E-MAIL.
LET ME TAKE A LOOK.
UH-HUH.
YEP.
I SEE NOW.
KLIK
KLIK
IT MAY HAVE SOMETHING TO DO WITH THE FACT THAT YOU ENDED OFF YOUR LAST E-MAIL WITH 'HEIL HITLER!'
WHAT???
YOU CHANGED MY YAHOO MAIL SIGNATURE!
IF THAT'S WHERE YOUR LOYALTIES LIE, YOU MIGHT WANT TO CHECK OUT ARYANROMANCE.COM
NOW WITH 97% LESS VERMIN.

TEACH A MAN

YOU KNOW WHAT'S A GOOD CURSE TO CALL SOMEONE?
FISH WHORE.
IT'S SOMEONE WHO HAS SEX WITH A FISH IN EXCHANGE FOR MONEY.
I GOT IT.
WHY YOU WALKING SO FAST?
FISH WHORE.

SIMPLY GOOD MANNERS

EXECUTIVE WASHROOM
HEY.
OH MY GOD-
I'M SORRY-
I DIDN'T-
SLAM
THAT'S MY BOY.
WAVE GOODBYE TO THE NICE LADY.

VANITY, THY NAME IS RAYNE

RAYNE FILED A COMPLAINT OVER WHAT HAPPENED THIS MORNING.
IN THE WASHROOM.
I DIDN'T DO IT ON PURPOSE!
I DIDN'T MEAN TO GRAB A GLIMPSE OF HIS-
HE'S NOT UPSET THAT YOU SAW HIS,
AND I QUOTE,
'INSTRUMENT OF INDESCRIBABLE ECSTASY'.
HE'S UPSET THAT YOU DIDN'T COMPLIMENT IT.
I'VE RAISED YOUR SALARY.
RETROACTIVE FROM THIS MORNING.

POLE POLL

HELLO. YOU.
I'M HOPING WE CAN SETTLE THIS MATTER RIGHT NOW.
WHAT YOU DID HURT ME ON A VERY PERSONAL LEVEL, NANCY.
FURTHERMORE, I'M NO LAWYER, OR A GUY WHO REGULARLY ADHERES TO 'LAWS',
BUT I'M PRETTY SURE THAT THIS FALLS UNDER SEXUAL HARASSMENT IN THE WORK PLACE.
NOW, I NEED YOU TO LOOK AT MY PENIS AGAIN AND GIVE ME YOUR FIRST IMPRESSIONS.
FOLLOWING THAT, I HAVE A SHORT SURVEY.
ONE EXTRA WEEK OF VACATION A YEAR.

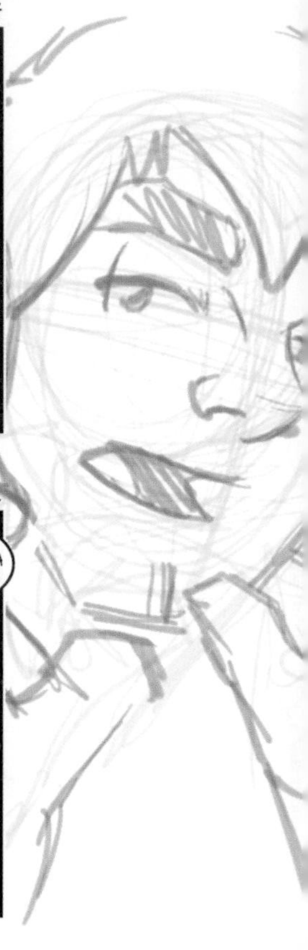

FULFILLING IN CREATIVE WAY

RAYNE-
I'M NOT LOOKING AT YOUR-
LET'S EVERYONE JUST RELAX.
NOW, WOULD YOU PLEASE JUST REVIEW MY JUNK SO WE CAN MOVE ON?
I BET BILL GATES DOESN'T HAVE TO DEAL WITH EMPLOYEES EXPOSING THEMSELVES.
YOU'RE RIGHT.
THIS IS UNFAIR OF ME.
MR GATES?
AN ODD AND VERY GRAPHIC FAX JUST CAME IN FOR YOU-
A MOMENT.
STEVIE J IS ALMOST DONE WITH THE VISTA SERVICE PACK.

PUPPET SHOW

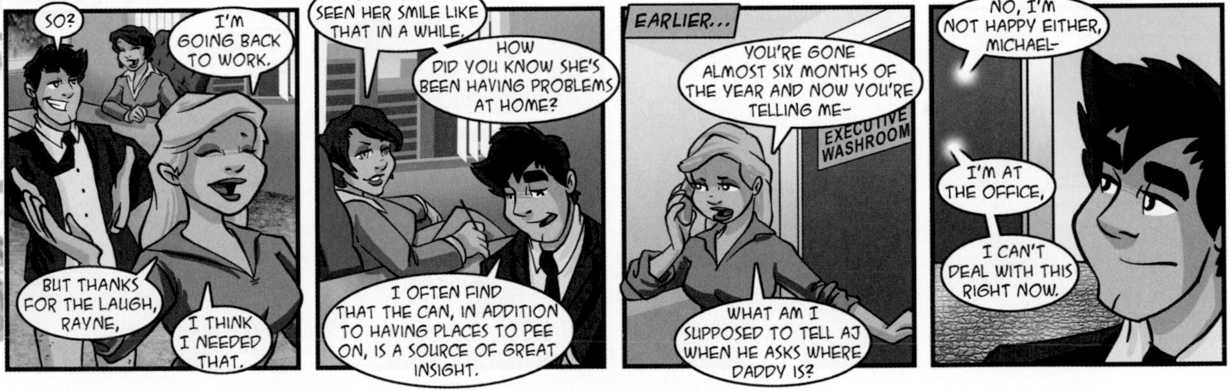
SO?
I'M GOING BACK TO WORK.
BUT THANKS FOR THE LAUGH, RAYNE,
I THINK I NEEDED THAT.
I HAVEN'T SEEN HER SMILE LIKE THAT IN A WHILE.
HOW DID YOU KNOW SHE'S BEEN HAVING PROBLEMS AT HOME?
I OFTEN FIND THAT THE CAN, IN ADDITION TO HAVING PLACES TO PEE ON, IS A SOURCE OF GREAT INSIGHT.
EARLIER...
YOU'RE GONE ALMOST SIX MONTHS OF THE YEAR AND NOW YOU'RE TELLING ME-
EXECUTIVE WASHROOM
WHAT AM I SUPPOSED TO TELL AJ WHEN HE ASKS WHERE DADDY IS?
NO, I'M NOT HAPPY EITHER, MICHAEL-
I'M AT THE OFFICE,
I CAN'T DEAL WITH THIS RIGHT NOW.

TWO BITS!

YOU KNOW SOMETIMES WHEN I'M TRYING TO MAKE A DECISION,
AND I TURN TO YOU AND ASK 'WHAT DO YOU THINK'?
YEAH.
I DON'T REALLY CARE WHAT YOU SAY.
I'M JUST BEING POLITE AND TRYING TO INCLUDE YOU.
YOU GET THAT, RIGHT?
WHAT DO YOU THINK?

SHORT BUS

WHAT HAS GOTTEN IN TO THE TWO OF YOU LATELY?
SORRY, MR GOLD.
SORRY.
Welcome class
1990
First day of school
HI.
I'M JOHN.
I FOUND SOMETHING NEAT IN MY PANTS TODAY.

VIOLENCE, EXCLUSION AND DEGRADATION

I LIKE FUZZY STICKERS.
THEY'RE FUZZY.
AND STICKYERY.
ME-
SPANG
YOU'RE IN THE WAY BABY.
OW.
AIEEEEE!
THANKS.
MOM'S RIGHT.
I NEED TO CHANGE MY UNDERWEAR MORE OFTEN.

SPONTANEOUS COMBUSTION

HI MOM!
THIS IS JOHN.
HE FOLLOWED ME HOME.
CAN I KEEP HIM?
HE MAY HAVE TO LEAVE EVENTUALLY, SWEETHEART.
DID THE TWO OF YOU HAVE A FUN DAY AT SCHOOL?
SOME GRADE SIXERS PICKED ON US.
JOHN SAID I SHOULDN'T SET THEM ON FIRE.
SO HE'S GOING TO BE THE VOICE OF REASON FROM NOW ON?
LESS TALKIE.
MORE BACK SCRATCHIE.

HAIR LIKE JEBAS WORE IT

GIMME A HEAD WITH HAIR
LONG BEAUTIFUL HAIR
SHINING, GLEAMING,
STREAMING, FLAXEN, WAXEN
HAIR!
THAT'S MY BROTHER ERIC
HE LIKES HIS HAIR A LOT.
HAIR!
HE'S ALSO A DOUCHE.
UH-HUH.
WHAT DOES THAT MEAN?
DUNNO.
BUT IT FEELS RIGHT, Y'KNOW?

BEE-EFF-EFF

I HAD FUN TODAY. WE SHOULD DO THIS AGAIN.
SURE.
WE'RE BEST FRIENDS NOW.
FOREVER.
FOREVER.
FOREVER.
HEY. STOP THAT.
FOREVER.
BY THE WAY,
THAT KID WHO PLAYED ME IN EPISODE ONE IS LESS OF A GIRL THAN YOU.

BLINK

Q AND A

WHAT'S YOUR PROBLEM LATELY?
JESUS MADE ME DO IT.
WHAT? NO-
I MEANT WHY HAVE YOU BEEN TREATING ME LIKE CRAP?
ALL YOU EVER DO IS PULL PRANKS AND HARASS ME.
WELL?
LET ME GUESS,
YOU'RE THINKING OF A CLEVER REPLY-
THOSE PRANKS ARE THE ONLY TIME WE'VE SPENT TOGETHER IN THE LAST TWO YEARS.

DER BUSENFREUND

YOU'VE WANTED TO SPEND MORE TIME WITH ME?
WHY WOULDN'T YOU JUST COMMUNICATE THAT INSTEAD OF ACTING OUT LIKE A FOUR YEAR OLD?
COMMUNICATE?
LIKE HOW I INVITED YOU TO NEW YORK CITY, LOS ANGELES, AND JAMAICA?
I WAS BUSY.
WERE YOU ALSO TOO BUSY TO COME TO MY CHARITY DINNER OR HELP NOEL MOVE?
OR VISIT ME IN THE GODDAMN HOSPITAL?
I COULDN'T...
YOU PUT **HEIL HITLER** ON THE BOTTOM OF MY E-MAILS!
ONE ISSUE AT A TIME.
WE CAN DISCUSS YOUR LOVE OF THE THIRD REICH A LITTLE LATER.

ONE POINT TWENTY-ONE

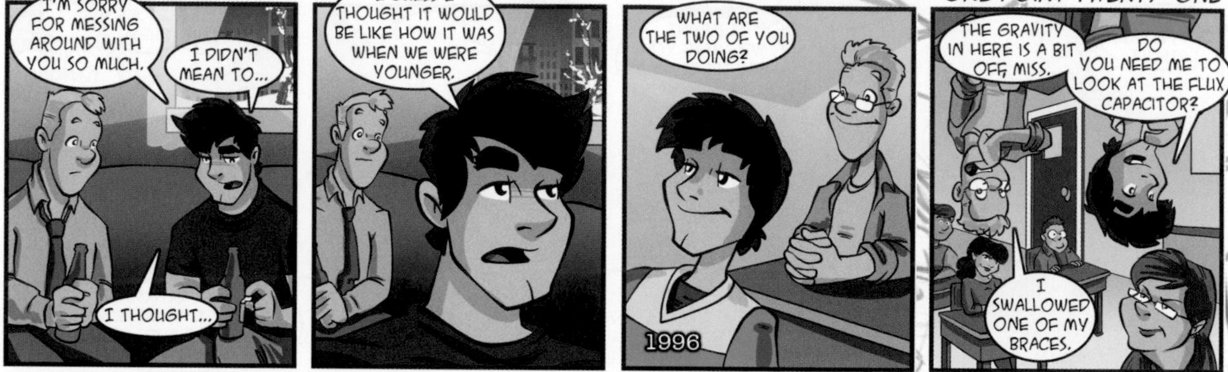

I'M SORRY FOR MESSING AROUND WITH YOU SO MUCH.
I DIDN'T MEAN TO...
I THOUGHT...
I GUESS I THOUGHT IT WOULD BE LIKE HOW IT WAS WHEN WE WERE YOUNGER.
WHAT ARE THE TWO OF YOU DOING?
1996
THE GRAVITY IN HERE IS A BIT OFF, MISS.
DO YOU NEED ME TO LOOK AT THE FLUX CAPACITOR?
I SWALLOWED ONE OF MY BRACES.

HE'S A RIGHTEOUS DUDE

ACK!
THBBPT!
MR. SUMMERS.
ENOUGH.
BUT HE'S CHOKING-
MR GOLD IS NOT THE ONE DISTURBING THE CLASS.
APOLOGIZE TO HIM OR YOU'RE GOING RIGHT TO THE PRINCIPAL'S OFFICE.
WELL PLAYED, YOU SON OF A BITCH.
MR. SUMMERS!

OH, I GOT A LIVE ONE HERE!
PLEASE BE CAREFUL WITH THE HCL, CLASS.
IT IS A HIGHLY CORROSIVE LIQUID.
PHYSICS & CHEMISTRY LAB
HCL FIGHT!
WAIT.
I THINK THAT'S TAKING IT TOO FAR.
FOR EVERY ACTION THERE IS AN EQUAL AND OPPOSITE REACTION.
HEY! YOU WERE LISTENING-
IN THIS CASE, THAT REACTION IS TO MELT YOUR FACE.
HOLD STILL AND I'LL TRY TO MAKE IT LIKE THE JOKER'S.
MR. SUMMERS!
3:10 TO WTF
1996
Gymnasium, Science Fair
AND WHAT HAVE YOU BOYS GOT FOR US TODAY?
WE CALL IT 'THE SUPER TRAIN!'
SUPER TRAI
IT LOOKS LIKE YOU TOOK A MODEL TRAIN AND GLUED ON WINGS.
TO THE UNEDUCATED, YES, I COULD SEE HOW THAT MIGHT BE PERCEIVED.
BUT LET ME ASSURE YOU, THAT SHOULD THIS TRAIN BE DE-RAILED DUE TO AN ACT OF GOD OR X-MEN, IT WILL SIMPLY GLIDE TO SAFETY.
MOVING ON.
WHAT IF YOUR MOM WAS ON THE TRAIN, DUDE?
DUDE?
YOUR MOM!

NO ONE MISSES DIAL-UP
WHAT DO YOU WANT TO DO TONIGHT?
I'M THINKING SCRAMBLED PORNO IS THE WAY TO GO.
I WAS PRETTY SURE I MADE OUT A BOOB LAST NIGHT.
I THOUGHT IT WAS A KNEE.
WHATEVER.
IT WAS NAKED.
WE COULD ALWAYS DOWNLOAD ANOTHER PAM ANDERSON PICTURE FROM THE INTERNET.
THAT WILL TAKE SIX HOURS.
LET'S GO BUY CONDOMS INSTEAD.
ALL THE KING'S HORSES
IT'S A FUNNY THING WHAT YOU CAN DO WITH INFORMATION.
FOR EXAMPLE, I HAPPEN TO KNOW WHERE OUR ENGLISH TEACHER LIVES.
I ALSO KNOW THAT I POSSESS AN EGG.
REMEMBER HOW YOU FELT BAD THE NEXT DAY AND WENT BACK TO CLEAN UP?
EXCEPT YOU FORGOT THE TEACHER'S ADDRESS AND CLEANED THE WRONG HOUSE?
DOING THAT LADY'S WINDOWS HELPED PUT ME THROUGH COLLEGE.

TRY NOT TO CLENCH

I'M SORRY FOR HOW I'VE BEEN BEHAVING LATELY.
INSTEAD OF ACTING OUT, I WILL VERBALIZE WHAT I'M FEELING.
LIKE A WOMAN.
I'M SORRY TOO.
I'VE BEEN SO SELF INVOLVED, THAT I HAVEN'T PAID MUCH ATTENTION TO ANYTHING ELSE.
ESPECIALLY YOU.
SO...
MAKE-UP SEX?
WHAT?
I MAY NOT KNOW MUCH ABOUT RELATIONSHIPS BUT I'M PRETTY SURE I'VE GOT THE RECONCILIATION PART RIGHT.
DON'T MAKE A BIG DEAL OF IT.
JUST TAKE OFF YOUR PANTS.

I TAWT I TAW

YOU KNOW THE EXPRESSION 'TIT FOR TAT'?
YEAH.
I KNOW WHAT A TIT IS.
BUT WHAT'S A 'TAT'?
WHAT'S A 'TAT'?
THERE GOES THE THEORY THAT WITH AGE COMES WISDOM.
TIT.

I'M A BIG KID NOW

OH FOR
SAKE.
YEAH, SO I'M DRIVING HERE,
STUCK IN TRAFFIC
WHEN ALL OF A SUDDEN I HAVE TO POOP REALLY, REALLY BAD.
I THINK I SERIOUSLY MIGHT CRAP MY PANTS.
YOU HAVE A CALL.
I AM NEVER ANSWERING YOUR PHONE AGAIN.

THINKING OUTSIDE THE BUNS

I DOUBLE PARKED MY CAR IN FRONT OF SOME RANDOM HIGH-RISE AND RAN IN AT RIDICULOUS SPEED.
SCREEE
TOLD THE SECURITY GUARD I HAD A MEETING WITH A MR. MORTENSEN.
I MANAGED TO FIND THE BATHROOM, IN THE DARKEST DEPTHS OF THE BUILDING.
IT WAS A GLORIOUS POOP.
HAAAAAH
A POOP THAT WILL BE TOLD AND RETOLD FOR GENERATIONS TO COME.
AFTERWARDS, IT HIT ME.
THERE WAS NO TOILET PAPER.
NO PAPER PRODUCTS AT ALL,
AND NO ONE WAS COMING TO MY RESCUE.
AND?
AND THAT'S WHEN I WIPED MY ASS WITH MY SCARF.